FROM HEAD TO TOE

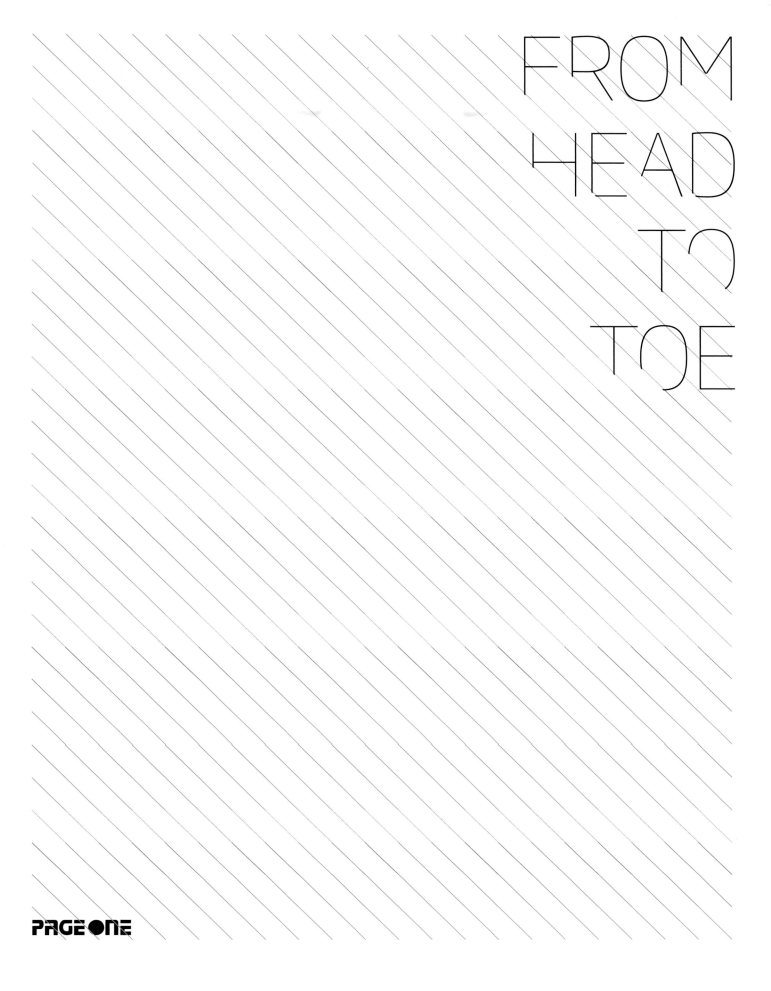

PAGE●ONE

FROM HEAD TO TOE
Copyright © 2009 by SANDU PUBLISHING

Published in Asia in 2009 by Page One Publishing Pte Ltd
20 Kaki Bukit View, Kaki Bukit Techpark II
Singapore 415956
Tel: (65) 6742-2088
Fax: (65) 6744-2088
enquiries@pageonegroup.com
www.pageonegroup.com

Sponsored by: Design 360°– Concept and Design Magazine
www.360indesign.com
Chief Editor: Wang Shaoqiang
Executive Editor: Mariah Lin
Design: Zhao Yu
Cover: Fashion by Kling by Kling, Photo by Studio SEEK
Sales Managers: Niu Guanghui (China), Daniela Huang (International)
Address: 3rd Floor, West Tower, No. 10 Ligang Road, Haizhu District,
510280, Guangzhou, China
Tel: (86)-20-84344460
Fax: (86)-20-84344460
sandu84344460@163.com
www.sandu360.com

ISBN 978-981-245-866-7

Printed and bound in China

Preface

Graphics is the art or the science of drawing, not really something that you can only see it, but also feel it, smell it, taste it, swallow it, and digest it. It is mixed of emotion, intuition, common sense and uncommon thinking; and it is carried out in the way of working interdisciplinary, colors, geometry, fine arts, and the relationship between numbers of those involved elements. Graphics focus on visual communication and presentation. Various methods are used to create and combine symbols, images and/or words to create a visual representation of ideas and messages. It can be as simple as a dot or a line, and those simple dots and lines make a beautiful scene.

Fashion is what we deal with everyday, a language which tells a story about the person who wears it, and a wordless way of communication that we all understand. It is a means of self-expression that allows people to try on many roles in life, and also a means of protecting oneself from exposing the true inside. The inspiration of fashion can be anything, music, flowers, food, animals, buildings, vehicles, furniture, etc. Fashion represents something forgettable, thrown away by time while running as fast as it can, trying not to be left behind. That is much like a circle, if you run too fast and try too hard, you will miss the best part of it.

Spring, summer, autumn, winter, four seasons of the year, change of color themes, keep life interesting and refresh feelings. Spring in pink sows seeds of love, new hope, joy and happiness. Grass breaking through the soil, leaves sprouting on the trees, animals rubbing their eyes coming out of hibernation, it is time to give birth to babies, and time to dance in the sparkling peak green path. Summer in green signifies growth, care, fantasies and passion, blooming flowers and rainbow after the rain. One can surf on the sunshine coast, watching and feeling for the wave and working hard to become part of it; or, take a nap under a flourishing small-leaved banyan, dreaming and leaving the ice-cream melting on the next table. Autumn in yellow brings maturity, harvest, cool breeze and bright moon, birds heading south, trees dropping leaves and blanketing the ground. Mornings seem darker and evenings come sooner. The scent of burning firewood has been detected, wafting along the house from the neighborhood in the countryside. Winter in grey illustrates a picture of snowfall, freezing lakes, energy drain and calm streets. But still, there is something to introspect and to hope for. Reading by the lamp until falling asleep with the Bible in the left hand on the white pillow, you are waiting for the loved one to come, or vaguely see that Santa Claus has just climbed down the chimney, not mere leaving a present but waking you up, inviting you to his reindeer sleigh.

Paola Ivana Suhonen, starting from her dark naive mind-landscapes, northern legends and sagas, designs prints, graphics, short movies, everything that is involved with visuals. Daniel Palillo, Finnish-Italian fashion designer working hard but without thinking too much, is distinct for its oversized baggy silhouette collections. With a background of graphic design, Frederique Daubal experiments with textile and lots of second hand pieces as a three-dimensional medium to create clothes without following any trends. Laurent Desgrange, creating a fantasized reality ruled by logic of his own, illustrates the mythology characters with a sense of joy and humor. Mathieu Missiaen, never happy with what he finished, always pushes a little bit further his art and ideas. Silvia Salvador and Nando Cornejo, Berlin based graphic and fashion designers draw inspiration from small details, contemporary and popular art in all its facets, folklore, street art, graffiti and music. Hoiming, creating bags with reasons and surprises, has its spirit which is to explore and to inspire, and its works recapture the essence of elegance in its own mischievous way. Sandor Lakatos, who made himself a T-shirt at the age of six, is a Hungary bespoke tailor and menswear designer, dedicating to create new cut which is never seen before. Emeli Martensson, gets her admirers who are fashionistas, punks, spoiled teenagers, moms in their 30's, hipsters, artists and musicians, unisex by making simple T-shirts with bold black prints, playing with famous logos like Chanel, Marc Jacobs, Collosseum, Tour Eiffel, etc. Przemek Sobocki, coming from a background of interior design, has developed his career in fashion illustration as the broadest means to express his love for arts. Three persons (DJ, designer and photographer) are doing graphic designs, photos, videos, organizing parties under the name of CHICKENSHIT, expecting more exhibitions, installations and new collaborations. Alba Brito Beaujon, attracted by all kinds of symbolism and influenced by advertising and campaign, illustrates on T-shirts and tote bags with great visual impact. Elena Gallen, combining naive, odd and minimalistic, draws inspiration from trash culture, cult movies, postmodernism, consumerism and an unusual taste for monsters. Hanna Werning has a strong fascination for patterns, and her work is all about great ideas and smart solutions with a visual attraction that makes people look and think. Uniforms for the Dedicated is put forth by creators with various creative backgrounds and ideas, of which the label serves as a platform for musicians, illustrators, designers, and more, thus creating a collective force of a widespread creative network. Martine Viergever, Dutch jewellery designer, believes that it is her role to lead fashion to different and unexpected ways and to be the one to change fashion constantly. Annalisa Dunn and Dorothee Hagemann, met on the MA Fashion course at Central St Martins in London founded knitwear label Cooperative Designs and has been creating modern innovative knitwear, subverting traditional techniques, silhouettes and forms. Karolina Kling, with a background in graphic design, has a unique take on fashion, both highly personal and yet commercial. Last but not least, the Gemini Graphic Artist Filip Pagowski falls in a gray area between graphics and the fine arts, and is amused by music, architecture, skiing, adventure, and women.

Nineteen designers from thirteen countries, with a professional knowledge background in graphic design or fashion design or both, will show you the most exciting and inspiring intimate relationships between fashion and graphics. In this book, not only can you experience visual impact, some crazy edgy stunning illustration while still wearable stylish fashion, but also you can find out how original concepts were developed to the final execution.

SPRING

SUMMER

Content

AUTUMN

WINTER

SPRING

Season of growth, speed and ideas; time for love of those fab new pairs of sandals; puffy clouds and lime-green leafs; song birds humming in every birch tree; long days and short sleeves; blushed cherry blossom cheeks; pale naked legs skipping down the streets; Smell of asphalt and unworn leather; Picking dandelions and finding a lost feather; wearing tight jeans in rainy showers; Losing one hour trying to fit into so last season print of flowers; the transition of winter into summer.

—Hanna Werning

TITLE: Lonely Tiger \ **FASHION**: IVANAhelsinki \ **GRAPHIC**: IVANAhelsinki \ **PHOTO**: IVANAhelsinki

DESCRIPTION: There is an old Russian folk legend about the world's saddest tiger. Tiger of Amur, once lived far, far away in the east, behind dark green endless taigas, and the foggy valley hills of Lake Baikal, was the king of his kingdom, the crown holder of his great Siberian Plateau land.

By evil accident he lost it all. Man hunter came to this Promised Land. His lady lover, queen of Tiger Land, wife of emperor turned into fur carpet, head remained as gadget of ones power. Kids were sold to Zoo, family of tigers scattered around human earth, bones for sale; balsam for healing hungry.

Sad Tiger, Lonely Tiger. Saddest Tiger in the wild world.

There he still lives and cries, alongside his sorrow water, in the shores of Tiger Tear Ponds.

TITLE: Fasan \ **FASHION**: IVANAhelsinki \ **GRAPHIC**: IVANAhelsinki \ **PHOTO**: IVANAhelsinki

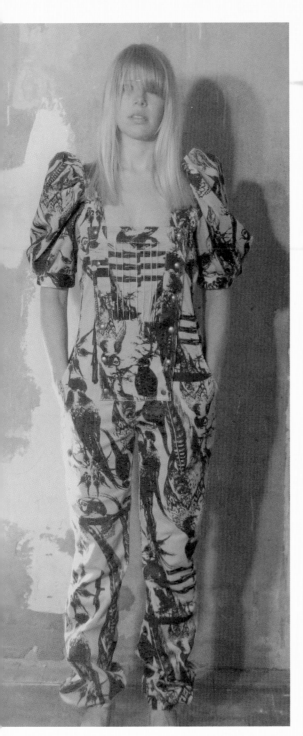

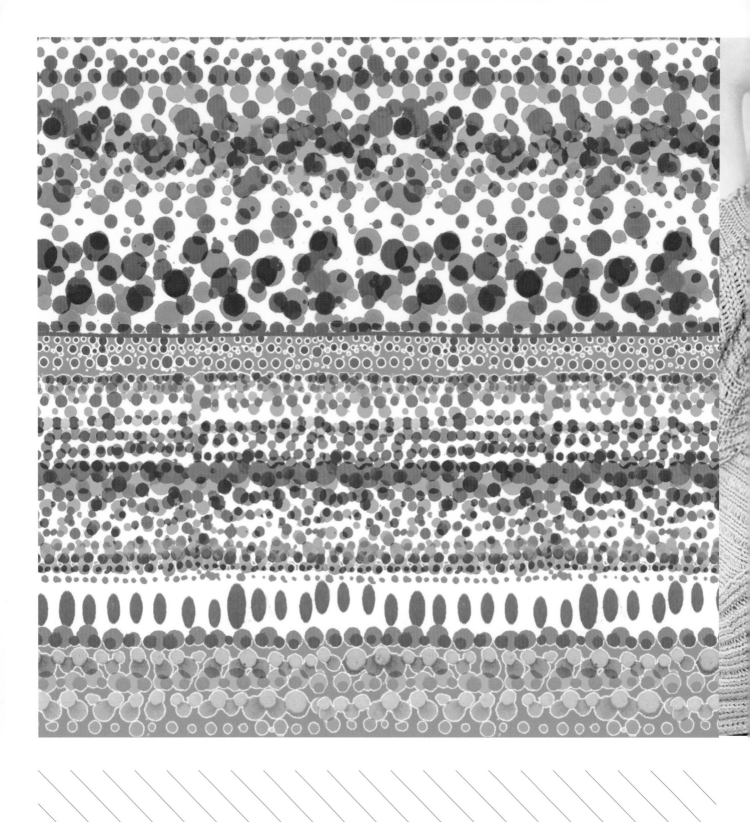

TITLE: Dot \ **FASHION**: House of Dagmar \ **GRAPHIC**: Hanna Werning \ **PHOTO**: House of Dagmar \ **YEAR**: 2008

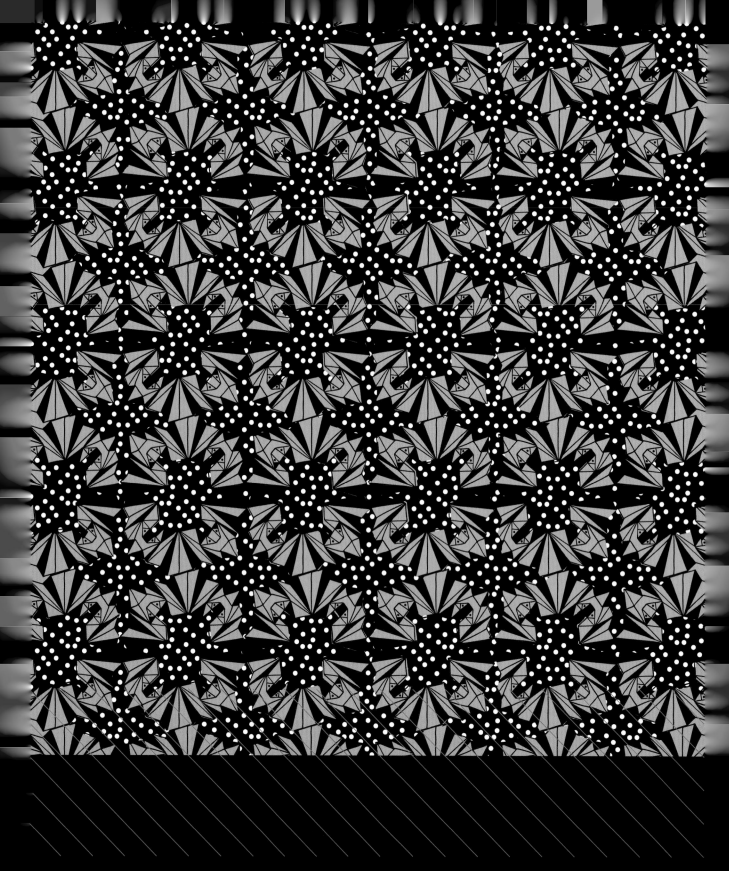

TITLE: SparKLING Nights   **FASHION**: Kling by Kling   **GRAPHIC**: Kling by Kling   **PHOTO**: Studio SEEK
STYLING: Emil Boström   **HAIR**: Emil Boström   **YEAR**: 2009
DESCRIPTION: The collection is based on stories by her closest friends, related to the sentence "sparKLING nights". Different

TITLE: Chestnut 3, Chestnut 1, Autumn Bits from the collection 'Season's Greetings' \ **Design**: Martine Viergever
PHOTO: Thomas Voorn \ **STYLING**: Thomas Voorn \ **MODEL**: Katinka \ **YEAR**: 2008
DESCRIPTION: The thematic clichés commonly used served as the starting point in designing this collection, plunging into autumn feelings for inspiration. Forest fruits are executed in silver and made into arrangements.

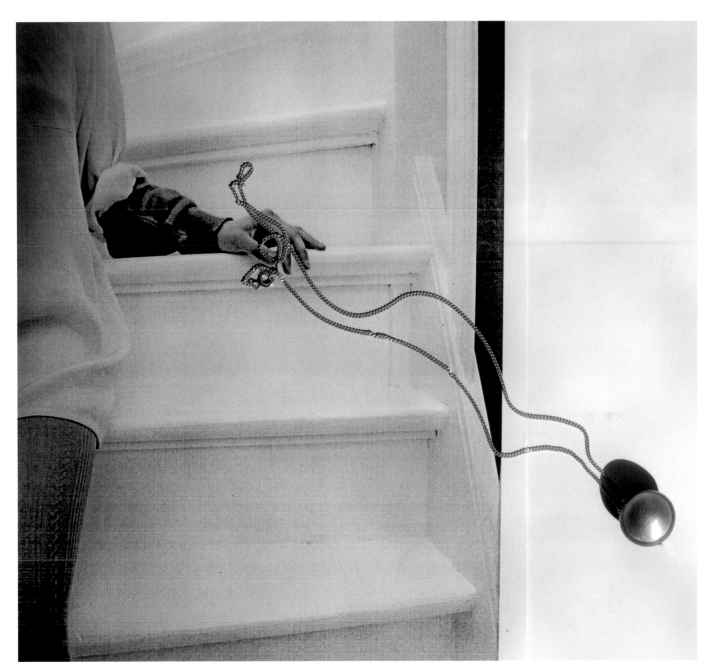

TITLE: Bird Ring   **FASHION**: IVANAhelsinki   **GRAPHIC**: IVANAhelsinki   **PHOTO**: Ivo Corda, IVANAhelsinki
DESCRIPTION: Not having been a big fan of mohair knits or animal skin look like materials, the designer wanted to see what the
metamorphosis was when going through the process starting with something she really disliked. In the end she was in love with the
same things. Bird Ring collection has a bit spooky 50's feeling with caged birds... what would happen to human beings if they were

TITLE: The Potipot Island Collection \ **FASHION**: potipoti \ **GRAPHIC**: Nando Cornejo & Silvia Salvador
PHOTO: Frank Kalero \ **STYLING**: Silvia S. Kopp \ **HAIR**: Loreal \ **MAKE-UP**: Loreal \ **MODEL**: Irene \ **YEAR**: 2009
DESCRIPTION: Surfing on the net they discovered a lost island in the Pacific Ocean called Potipot. This finding, together with a
recent trip to Costa Rica, inspired them to produce a very exotic and tropical collection.
Their goal is to eventually conquer Potipot Island and live there for ever, drinking avocado milkshakes and having a good time.
Prints remind indigenous cabins, bamboo, palm trees, volcanoes and ancestral monsters.
For this summer collection they have used light and fresh fabrics like silk, cotton, linen

TITLE: SparKLING Nights   FASHION: Kling by Kling   GRAPHIC: Kling by Kling   PHOTO: Studio SEEK

TITLE: Mod. Cavour Black Oversize \ **GRAPHIC**: 5PREVIEW \ **PHOTO**: Giorgia Placidi \ **STYLING**: Emeli Martensson
MODEL: Greta \ **YEAR**: 2009
DESCRIPTION: Oversize black tanktop from the THIRD COLLECTION.

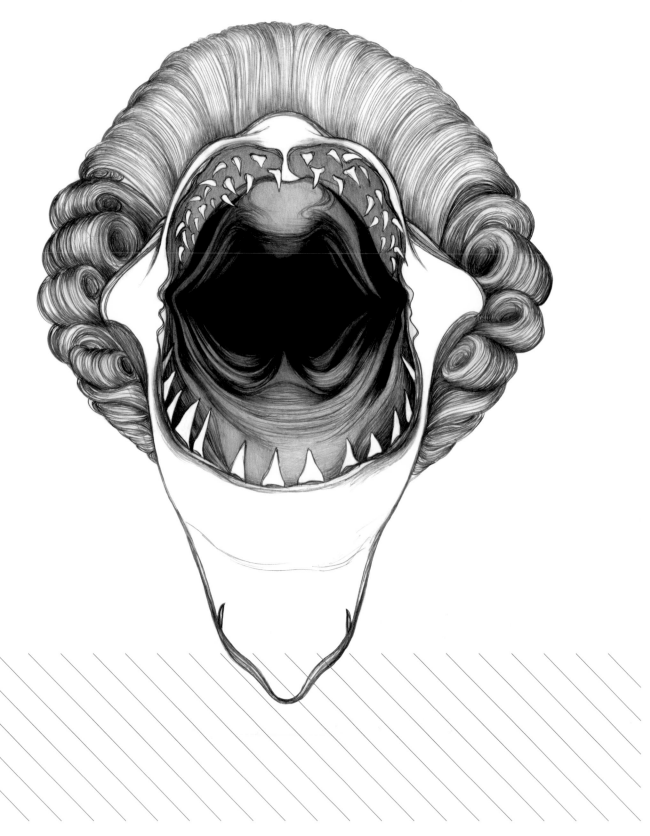

TITLE: The Gardens of O.D.P \ **ART DIRECTION**: Daniel Palillo \ **FASHION**: Daniel Palillo
GRAPHIC: Laura Laine, Daniel Palillo \ **PHOTO**: Paavo Lehtonen \ **STYLING**: Henna Koskinen
MODEL: Laura and Marko \ **YEAR**: 2009
DESCRIPTION: Ice hockey players mixed with baroque.

TITLE: Flower anad pattern \ **GRAPHIC**: Ndeur \ **PHOTO**: Camille Verrier \ **STYLING**: Ndeur & Camille Verrier
MODEL: Kevin Galaccio \ **YEAR**: 2008
DESCRIPTION: Pattern kin of futuristic ethnic, the first pair of sneakers in the designer's history. The inspiration was a lot focus on the black and white pattern and the cheesy kind of look of the flower, which he loves playing with the border between good and bad taste.

TITLE: We Are All the Best \ **FASHION**: Frederique Daubal \ **GRAPHIC**: Frederique Daubal \ **PHOTO**: Frederique Daubal
STYLING: Frederique Daubal \ **YEAR**: 2008
DESCRIPTION: With a handmade rosette ribbon, becoming the best.

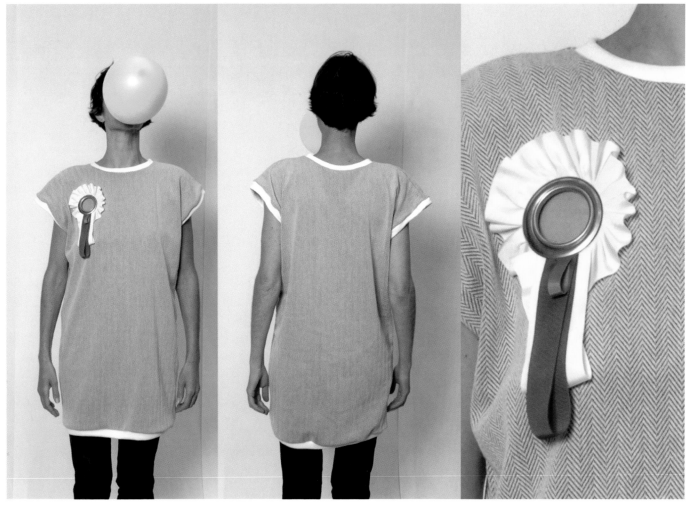

TITLE: Shape Sweat \ **FASHION**: Frederique Daubal \ **GRAPHIC**: Frederique Daubal \ **PHOTO**: Johanna Salomez
STYLING: Frederique Daubal \ **YEAR**: 2008
DESCRIPTION: The goal was to remove all spots or used pieces of fabric and to replace them by another fabric, a way to recycle the garment.

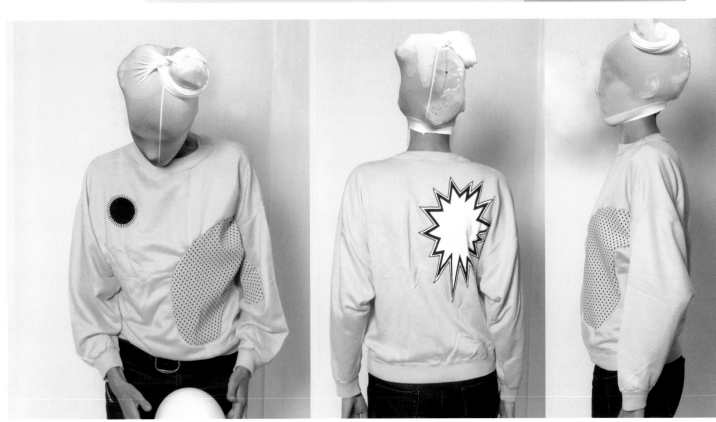

TITLE: Twins Shirt \ **FASHION**: Frederique Daubal \ **GRAPHIC**: Frederique Daubal \ **PHOTO**: Frederique Daubal
STYLING: Frederique Daubal \ **YEAR**: 2008
DESCRIPTION: Meeting and mixing between two persons visualized in a shirt.

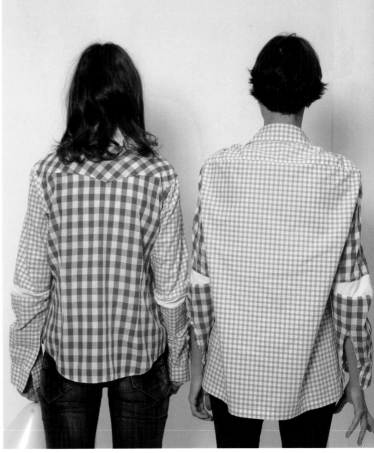

TITLE: Top-Top \ **FASHION**: Frederique Daubal \ **GRAPHIC**: Frederique Daubal \ **PHOTO**: Johanna Salomez
STYLING: Frederique Daubal \ **YEAR**: 2008
DESCRIPTION: What the difference between a top and a skirt or a skirt and a top.

TITLE: The Gardens of O.D.P \ **Art Direction**: Daniel Palillo \ **FASHION**: Daniel Palillo
GRAPHIC: Laura Laine, Daniel Palillo \ **PHOTO**: Paavo Lehtonen \ **STYLING**: Henna Koskinen
MODEL: Laura and Marko \ **YEAR**: 2009
DESCRIPTION: Ice hockey players mixed with baroque.

TITLE: The Gardens of O.D.P \ **ART DIRECTION**: Daniel Palillo \ **FASHION**: Daniel Palillo
GRAPHIC: Laura Laine, Daniel Palillo \ **PHOTO**: Paavo Lehtonen \ **STYLING**: Henna Koskinen
MODEL: Laura and Marko \ **YEAR**: 2009
DESCRIPTION: Ice hockey players mixed with baroque.

TITLE: Cocktail Collaboration ╲ **FASHION**: FouR ╲ **GRAPHIC**: Przemek Sobocki ╲ **PHOTO**: Maciej Kucia
STYLING: Maciejka ╲ **MODEL**: Joanna (MYSKENA) ╲ **YEAR**: 2008
DESCRIPTION: Special collaboration between Przemek Sobocki, FouR and Cocktail boutique /part of Sidefame in Hong Kong.
The designs by Przemek Sobocki were supposed to "show" the mood of Coctail Boutiques and their women customers; the idea
was to have one design/idea and its variation to make 4 different patterns.

TITLE: Fishpond Flush, Ocean Star, Grasshopper Luck \ **FASHION**: Eastpak \ **GRAPHIC**: Hanna Werning
PHOTO: Hanna Werning \ **YEAR**: 2005
DESCRIPTION: Intuitive flora and fauna colleges.

TITLE: Pinocchio Collection \ **DESIGN**: Hoiming Fung & Baldwin Pui \ **PHOTO**: Jacky Chee \ **YEAR**: 2009
DESCRIPTION: An impression between real and unreal, the collection is finely handmade of cork and leather. Make a little

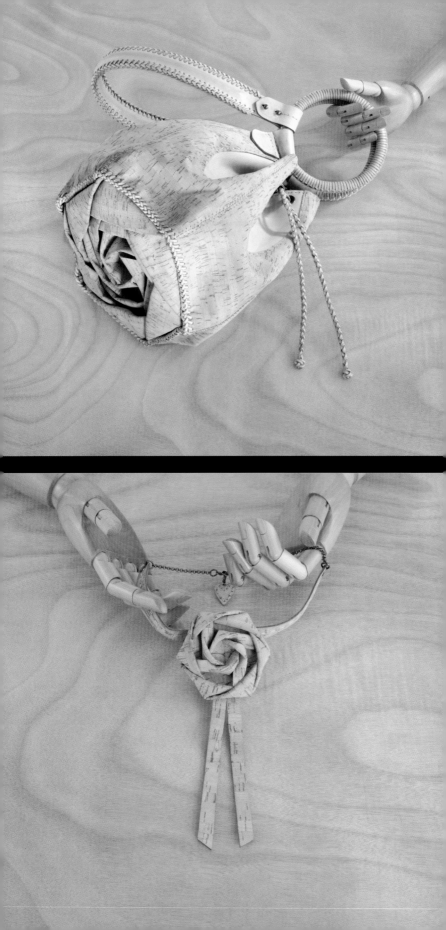

TITLE: Mod. 55 \ **GRAPHIC**: 5PREVIEW \ **PHOTO**: Giorgia Placidi \ **STYLING**: Emeli Martensson
MODEL: Greta \ **YEAR**: 2009
DESCRIPTION: Watercolor and ink illustration by Emeli for 5preview for WEEKDAY, white mod. 55 T-shirt from the THIRD
COLLECTION, black plexiglas pendant.

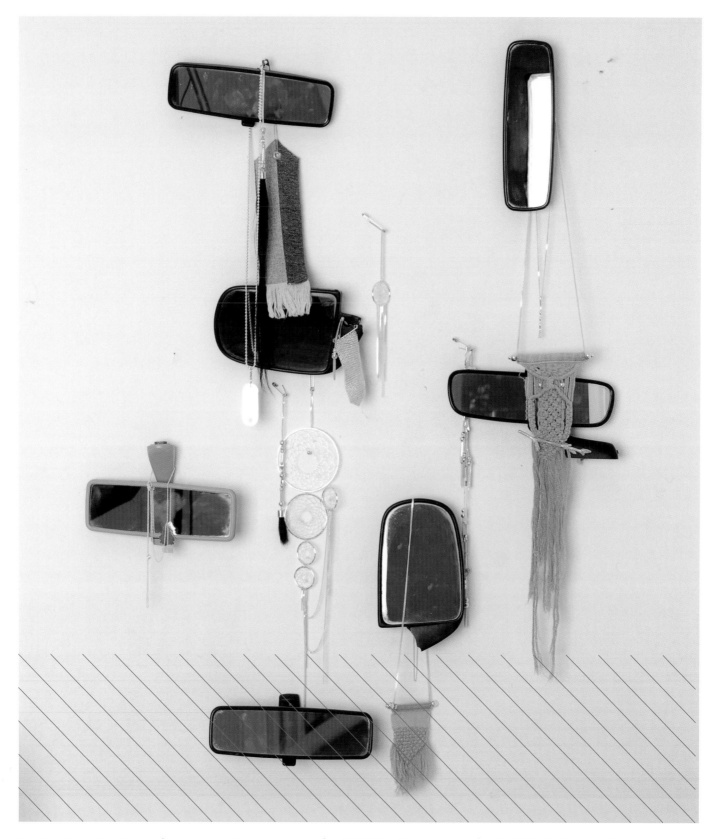

TITLE: Rear View Mirror \ **Design**: Martine Viergever \ **PHOTO**: Thomas Voorn \ **STYLING**: Thomas Voorn
MODEL: Amanda \ **YEAR**: 2009
DESCRIPTION: 'Rear View Mirror' is a collection inspired by car jewels, executed in silver and jeans. It expresses the thin line between individuality and mass product within the context of the rear view mirror. The rear view mirror serves as a peg for a variety of objects which will give the dashboard of the car a personal touch. Right above the control panel, with which the driver determines his way, amulets and mascots dangle. They guard for danger, stipulate for football prosperity and dissipate bad spirits and smells.

leftover
dressing gown
re-cut
as a jacket

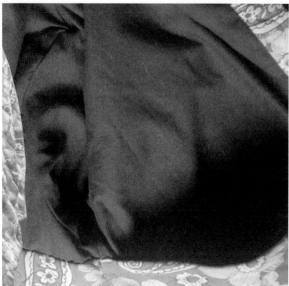

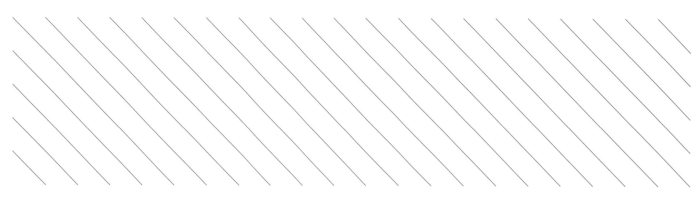

TITLE: Blue Warmer \ **FASHION**: Frederique Daubal \ **GRAPHIC**: Frederique Daubal \ **PHOTO**: Johanna Salomez
STYLING: Frederique Daubal \ **MODEL**: Tony and Lola and Romain \ **YEAR**: 2007
DESCRIPTION: Transformation of a heavy dressing gown into a little jacket

TITLE: potipoti glasses \ **DESIGN**: Maribel Pérez & potipoti \ **PHOTO**: Nando Cornejo \ **YEAR**: 2007
DESCRIPTION: potipoti glasses for a catwalk

INTERVIEW

IVANAhelsinki \ Finland

IVANAhelsinki is a Finnish art brand. It brings delicately together Slavic rough melancholy and pure Scandinavian moods with white arctic summer nights and endless winter sadness.
Paola Ivana Suhonen is the designer behind the fashion pieces, starting from her dark naive mind-landscapes, northern legends and sagas, doing prints, graphics, short movies and well, everything that is involved with visuals. She runs the family-owned indie flavored company with her older sister Pirjo. Every single IVANAhelsinki piece is manufactured in Finland. The whole production philosophy is based on ethical and ecological choices. There are a lot of handmade details and traditional Finnish handcraft methods are featured.

F \ The Finnish art brand IVANAhelsinki brings delicately together Slavic rough melancholy and pure Scandinavian moods with white arctic summer nights and endless winter sadness. What was the romantic story behind the brand?
I \ Romantic story? We tell stories, that's our story. For me the whole working method is like living in my own dream world and then choosing one path to follow each season. I follow my own instinct, behaving like a kid in a candy store. I choose the amount of the dresses, just a random number, because I'm pretty much number obsessed and it helps me to concentrate and not disappear to my own mad layers. I design that amount of "best of" dresses under certain theme/story. I couldn't care less about the silhouettes/ trends, I just want to make a montage of the ones I would love to wear. Because I will never be "fashion accepted". I don't choose the safe and excepted trend lines. I always worry about that people REALLY hate me and my line this year. Every year the same pattern happens to me, heh.

F \ What is the weather like in Helsinki? Which season gives you the most inspiration?
I \ Helsinki is full of negative climates—dark, harsh winters, endless light and pale summer days. I personally love autumn. It is time for melancholy and it is like living in a visual poet.

F \ The prints, graphics, short movies created by IVANAhelsinki are so classically elegant and full of fantasy. What does fashion mean to you?
I \ It is more like a tool for expressing my own twisted universe. I feel that fashion itself is a bit worn-out and a boring concept. If you just try to create fashion, you are not doing anything experimental and pushing boarders further. It is like a painter who just colored or filled up the canvas but not tried to create something of his own. Fashion should be more expressionist, and that is the new wave of using it as a tool for your own experiments.

F \ As Ivana confessed that her dark naive mind-landscapes drove her to do cute, straight cotton and woolen dresses for charismatic drummer girls who are just after a love of their lives, waiting to see, will he be a rock-star, a motorbiker, a cosmonaut or a sailor. Is Ivana one of those girls?
I \ 100% yes.

F \ Did you enjoy your last attendance in the Paris Fashion Week? What is now your clients/audience looking for?
I \ Paris is always beautiful. Yes, I got really drunk with my sister. It was cool to see each others. Now I live in New York and my sister runs our factory back home in Helsinki. So yes, the attendance was great! I think my audience is looking for something bold, brave, savvy, bohemian, chic and intelligent. I really try to full fill their expectations. We are going to have some lost circus girls on a lonely highway!

F \ Where did you see the opportunity that the fashion industry lacks but you have?
I \ You have to be a visual gambler, romantic hard worker, aesthetic vagabond with passion and madness, and yeah, have a bit gipsy blood combined with Slavic rawness and have guardian angel above you. I have been lucky to have one.

Frédérique Daubal \ France

After being a foreigner in different countries, mainly Montreal and The Nederlands, Frédérique Daubal is now biking in Paris. Coming from a graphic design background, she also experiments with textile as a three-dimensional medium, or creates clothes under her name, without following any trends but using lots of second hand pieces since the beginning of 2001. She works as a freelance creative designer for clients worldwide, Nike, Paul Smith, Nokia, Publicis, Bumble & Bumble, etc. Daubal constantly collaborates with people and magazines for experimental ideas, installation or art direction in the related fields.

F \ You have been to different countries, Montreal, the Nederlands and Paris. Where did you start your graphic design and get inspired the most?
D \ I started in France but most inspiration came when I was abroad. Certainly because I felt more free and curious than in my own country, not secure and stable, always in the back of the mind to go against somewhere else. It might be totally psychological but it helped me a lot to go further in creativity. Staying in Montreal as a student, it was one of my best memories and brought me to another level of understanding in graphic design. And then working in the Nederlands can just kick out your creativity. Paris is less fun but more challenging to stay creative. Great people are everywhere anyways.

F \ How do you like designing clothes with second hand pieces and what was the idea behind Leftovers?
D \ There are different ways to enjoy it, but finding clothes already used by anonymous give me the energy to give another life to it. For sure money is not the clue, only personal pleasure animated by the joy to propose these garments to people. This kind of creation needs to be more exposed.
"Leftovers", I like that beautiful word in English. Making creation with the part of things we don't want, feeling like a stranger in a new surrounding. I see my creations like sketching ideas which has no ending.

F \ Your designs include typeface, illustration, editorial, products, installation, etc. Where does the dynamic energy and diversity come from?
D \ I guess it's easier to diversify the creativity by doing different disigns than trying to do the same things again and again. That is a good balance in my life.

F \ When you work for your clients, what do you think is the most important to finish a commission?
D \ Be convinced as much as the clients but may be not for the same reasons.

F \ Were you trained to be creative or born to be innovative?
D \ Who knows...

Przemek Sobocki \ Poland

Przemek Sobocki is specialized in fashion and interior design, graduated from the renowned Academy of Fine Arts, Wroclaw, Poland. He has developed his career in illustration as the broadest means to express his love for the arts -- film, photography, architecture, animation, literature, fashion, and design.

His illustrations for the brands such as Adidas, Undercover, Prada, Marc Jacobs and Balenciaga have been published in various international magazines. Przemek has had several successful exhibitions in the UK, Poland and Japan, where he currently resides.

F \ What is the connection between interior design and fashion illustration?

P \ Interior design is quite close to architecture. It is a pretty obvious relation between fashion and architecture, because both are based on "construction". My work is not really just a scrabbling on the piece of paper; it is more about planning to achieve certain result.

F \ What made you so passionate about fashion illustration?

P \ I have been drawing a lot and part of my diploma was a set of big drawings. When I got my first publication I decided to focus on this as part of my career. When I received V&A illustration award for best editorial 2005, I was convinced that I was on the right way. It gives me lots of freedom in terms what and how I want to express myself, making it I don't necessarily involve other people in the project, I don't need to be attached to one place, and I can use my fashion and interior background.

F \ What was the idea behind FouR?

P \ I was told that fashion in Japan is changing so quickly. Around each 2 years and its always big demand for new thing. So I wanted to create this 2 years brand, which has 4 collections, and then to change a bit concept for another 2 years. We even decided to change our logo every 2 years and even the logo is changing slightly each season which makes you easy to read which collection it is. Above the seasons then you can mix different collection together. It is more like a timeless collection.

F \ You have done a lot of projects in Hong Kong. How did you book the first one?

P \ One Japanese company organized for few brands from Japan a little exhibition for HK buyers in HK about 2 years ago. I knew a few people there already and met new ones of course. People from Cocktail boutique came and later they ordered part of my first collection "London".

F \ You have been working in Poland, London and Tokyo for years. Is the working environment very different in these three countries?

P \ It is not much about the working environment as I live in those three countries where I have been so inspired. As an illustrator I am working only in London and Japan, while in Poland I am an interior designer. Of course each project is different and there are some differences between markets but usually my style is not necessary to be adjusted to the demands of the market.

F \ What is your most recent discovery in life?

P \ Hmmm... May be that you always want to become somebody or go somewhere, but you can't tell. You are always searching to find out what life is and the answer is always far away.

SUMMER

Warm wind through while I'm sitting on the boat with my naked feet in the cold salty water... Seagulls screaming as I pass by the small stony islands... The huge white sail above me and my dad whistling at the stern behind me, mosquito-bites on tanned legs, freckles on my face. That's real summer.

—Emeli Martensson

TITLE: Dead Butterfly \ **FASHION**: IVANAhelsinki \ **GRAPHIC**: IVANAhelsinki \ **PHOTO**: Nina Merikallio, IVANAhelsinki

TITLE: Balletto \ **FASHION**: House of Dagmar \ **GRAPHIC**: Hanna Werning \ **PHOTO**: House of Dagmar
YEAR: 2009
DESCRIPTION: Inspired the Ingemar Bergman film "Sommaren med Monika" and ballet dancers in motion.

TITLE: SparKLING Nights \ **FASHION**: Kling by Kling \ **GRAPHIC**: Kling by Kling \ **PHOTO**: Studio SEEK
STYLING: Emil Boström \ **HAIR**: Emil Boström \ **YEAR**: 2009
DESCRIPTION: The collection is based on stories by her closest friends, related to the sentence "sparKLING nights". Different elements from their stories are then being applied into her graphics, appearing as allover patterns, covering every piece in the collection, combining a sense of elegant rococo with futuristic street ware.

TITLE: The Potipot Island Collection \ **FASHION**: potipoti, shoes KTW for potipoti
GRAPHIC: Nando Cornejo & Silvia Salvador \ **PHOTO**: Frank Kalero **STYLING**: Silvia S. Kopp \ **HAIR**: Loreal
MAKE-UP: Loreal \ **YEAR**: 2009
DESCRIPTION: Surfing on the net they discovered a lost island in the Pacific Ocean called Potipot. This finding, together with a recent trip to Costa Rica, inspired them to produce a very exotic and tropical collection. Prints remind indigenous cabins, bamboo, palm trees, volcanoes and ancestral monsters.

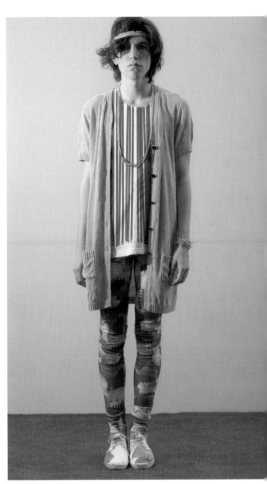

TITLE: The Gardens of O.D.P \ **Art Direction**: Daniel Palillo \ **FASHION**: Daniel Palillo
GRAPHIC: Laura Laine, Daniel Palillo \ **PHOTO**: Paavo Lehtonen \ **STYLING**: Henna Koskinen
MODEL: Laura and Marko \ **YEAR**: 2009
DESCRIPTION: Ice hockey players mixed with baroque.

TITLE: Kentuckyfriedchanel, Moccanorexia, Blessed Virgin, Terry Shoot \ **GRAPHIC**: Alba Brito for Dismissed
PHOTO: Ivan Llamas \ **STYLING**: Alba Brito \ **MAKE-UP**: Erica Mann \ **MODEL**: Barbara Masiá \ **YEAR**: 2008
DESCRIPTION: Colonel Saunders is part of a well known logotype, if you see him without the KFC abbreviation you would
know for sure who is it. Sunglasses, white ponytail, high-necked shirt has turned Mr. Lagerfeld into an icon for mainstream
fashion, and everybody will recognize him though he denounces french fries. Both faces helps us to visualize a company. And both
companies are very powerful and rich, either one represents wealth and the other trash.

TITLE: NEW YORK CITY and A BIG MONKEY, TWO ＼ **FASHION**: FouR ＼ **GRAPHIC**: Przemek Sobocki
PHOTO: Maciej Kucia ＼ **STYLING**: przem.ko ＼ **MODEL**: Shingo Yasuda ＼ **YEAR**: 2007
DESCRIPTION: Fourth and last collection of the Cities series called: NEW YORK CITY and a Big Monkey; inspirations: New York and all that was found fascinated. It s life, architecture and ... King Kong

FASHION: Uniforms for the Dedicated \ **GRAPHIC**: Johan Idesjö \ **PHOTO**: Peter Nilsson \ **YEAR**: 2009
DESCRIPTION: The illustrations tell the story how music shapes environments. As a result the illustrations are oceans of various motions and emotions.

TITLE: The Gardens of O.D.P \ **Art Direction**: Daniel Palillo \ **FASHION**: Daniel Palillo
GRAPHIC: Laura Laine, Daniel Palillo \ **PHOTO**: Paavo Lehtonen \ **STYLING**: Henna Koskinen
MODEL: Laura and Marko \ **YEAR**: 2009
DESCRIPTION: Ice hockey players mixed with baroque.

TITLE: The Gardens of O.D.P \ **Art Direction**: Daniel Palillo \ **FASHION**: Daniel Palillo
GRAPHIC: Laura Laine, Daniel Palillo \ **PHOTO**: Paavo Lehtonen \ **STYLING**: Henna Koskinen
MODEL: Laura and Marko \ **YEAR**: 2009
DESCRIPTION: Ice hockey players mixed with baroque.

TITLE: Toile de Jouy **GRAPHIC**: Laurent Desgrange **PHOTO**: Farrah Hammadou **MODEL**: Paul & Arsène
YEAR: 2009
DESCRIPTION: Party Animals

TITLE: Borderline Compass, Telephone Bird \ **FASHION**: Anna Sui \ **GRAPHIC**: Hanna Werning \ **PHOTO**: Anna Sui
YEAR: 2008
DESCRIPTION: Inspired the Wiener Werkstadt.

TITLE: Bowties & Pimp Your Sneakers bow ties \ **GRAPHIC**: Laurent Desgrange \ **PHOTO**: Laurent Desgrange
YEAR: 2008-2009
DESCRIPTION: Fun-street hommage to Louis XIV.

TITLE: A Surreal Future \ **GRAPHIC**: Laurent Desgrange \ **PHOTO**: Olivier Schwartz \ **STYLING**: Laurent Desgrange
MODEL: Romain \ **YEAR**: 2008
DESCRIPTION: The surface was in the Air.

TITLE: Mod. Cartoon \ **GRAPHIC:** 5PREVIEW PHOTO, Giorgia Placidi \ **STYLING:** Emeli Martensson \ **MODEL:** Greta
YEAR: 2009
DESCRIPTION: White T-shirt mod. CARTOON from the THIRD COLLECTION, ink illustration by Emeli, lyrics by Minor Threat.

IT'S LIKE SCREAMING AT A WALL
SOMEDAY   IT'S GONNA
                      FALL

YOU BETTER REINFORCE THOSE WALLS
UNTIL YOU DON'T HAVE NO ROOM
TO STAND 'CAUSE SOMEDAY THE BRICKS ARE GONNA FALL
SOMEDAY I'M GONNA   USE MY HANDS

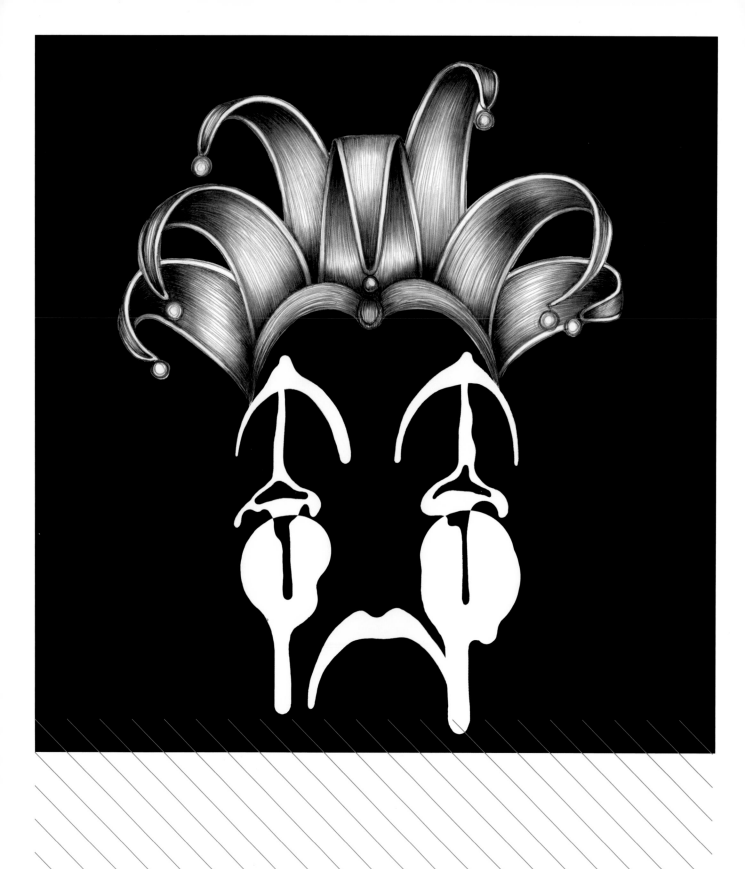

TITLE: The Gardens of O.D.P \ **Art Direction**: Daniel Palillo \ **FASHION**: Daniel Palillo
GRAPHIC: Laura Laine, Daniel Palillo \ **PHOTO**: Paavo Lehtonen \ **STYLING**: Henna Koskinen
MODEL: Laura and Marko \ **YEAR**: 2009
DESCRIPTION: Ice hockey players mixed with baroque.

TITLE: PORTRAITS, LONDON \ **FASHION**: FouR \ **GRAPHIC**: Przemek Sobocki \ **PHOTO**: Pi \ **STYLING**: przem.ko
MODEL: Aleksandra Ubukata \ **YEAR**: 2007

TITLE: Men's spring_summer2003(CdG) \ **FASHION**: Filip Pagowski \ **GRAPHIC**: Filip Pagowski \ **YEAR**: 2003

TITLE: Pigeon Pine \ FASHION: Anna Sui \ GRAPHIC: Hanna Werning \ PHOTO: Anna Sui \ YEAR: 2008

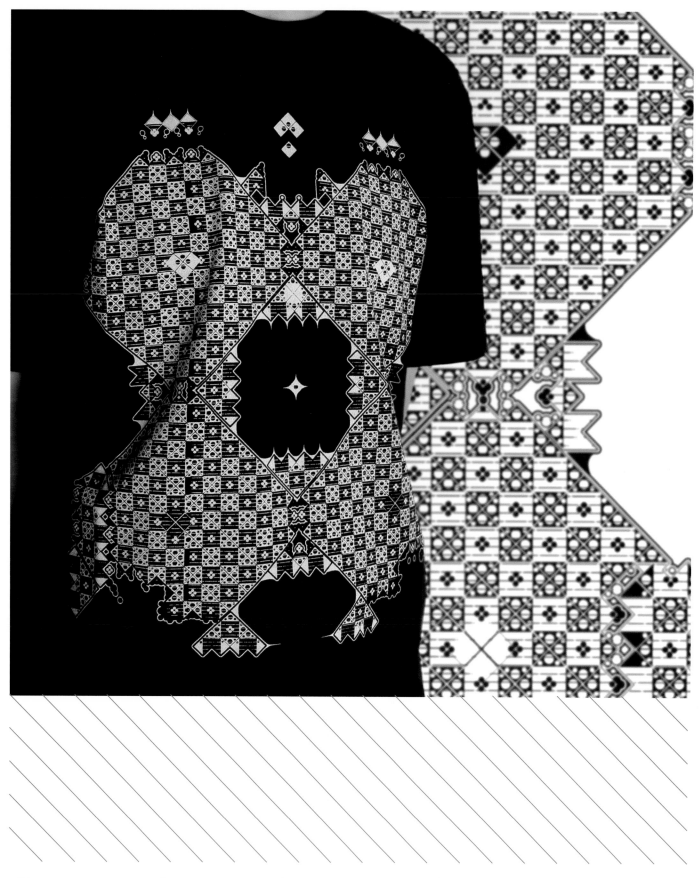

TITLE: T-shirts for Coltesse \ **GRAPHIC**: Ndeur \ **PHOTO**: Camille Verrier \ **STYLING**: Ndeur & Camille Verrier
MODEL: Adam Cruishanck \ **YEAR**: 2008
DESCRIPTION: Playing with the pattern and using them as volume and shape in a really futuristic way but always with a strong base of ethnic reference, the series of 4 exclusive tee-shirts were designed in a collector edition.

TITLE: Vans for Milo shoes gallery ＼ **DESIGN**: Ndeur ＼ **PHOTO**: Camille Verrier ＼ **STYLING**: Ndeur & Camille Verrier
YEAR: 2008
DESCRIPTION: Trying to go deeper and deeper in minimalism, pairs of sneakers were born.

TITLE: Shoes for Shibuya Trade Show \ **GRAPHIC**: Ndeur \ **PHOTO**: Camille Verrier
STYLING: Ndeur & Camille Verrier \ **YEAR**: 2008
DESCRIPTION: The pair on the left took the designer three full days of work, longest time in history. As simple in the shape but always with the same reference, including a bit of animal shape and maybe more Egyptian or Inca influence as the pair on the right, those were kind of a strange mix.

TITLE: Midsummer \ **FASHION**: House of Dagmar \ **GRAPHIC**: Hanna Werning \ **PHOTO**: House of Dagmar
YEAR: 2007
DESCRIPTION: Inspired by the Swedish Midsummer, the longest day of the year, when the nights are scarcely dark. The festive day and evening when you pick seven flowers and put them underneath your pillow to dream about your love to be.

TITLE: CHICKENSHIT by KNOTAN \ **GRAPHIC**: Chickenshit \ **PHOTO**: KNOTAN
MODEL: Hege, Torbjorn, KNOTAN \ **YEAR**: 2009
DESCRIPTION: Hege is famous Norwegian model; Torbjorn is band leader of Folke; Knotan is fashion photographer from Sweden.

TITLE: LEGENDA \ **GRAPHIC**: Chickenshit \ **PHOTO**: Artem Gavrilyuk \ **STYLING**: KNOTAN
MODEL: Artur \ **YEAR**: 2009
DESCRIPTION: Artur from music band "COLDOWN"

INTERVIEW

Hanna Werning \ Sweden

Hanna Werning established her own studio in 2004 in Stockholm working with self-initiated and commissioned work. Hanna has a strong fascination for patterns, whether it is the natural pattern of wood or something made-up and decorative.
She was educated a graphic designer at St. Martins College in London and has since then been designing prints, wallpapers, porcelain etc for the likes of IKEA, Boråstapeter, Rörstrand, Eastpak, Anna Sui and House of Dagmar. She wants her work to be based on ideas but always with an intuitive touch. Her aim is to be visually challenging but inviting.

F \ What is your working environment like?
H \ I have a studio in the centre of Stockholm and small workspace at home. I tend to work most creatively in the evening so that's why it is good to have a space at home. I have also bought a big and cheap former chapel in the countryside in the south of Sweden. It has a big space with high sealing where I am planning to have a summer studio in the future.

F \ Where does your creativity come from?
H \ When I get a new project I start a treasure hunt. I don't know what I am looking for in the beginning. I research through my old drawers; I visit the library; I look up related words in the glossary; I walk in the nature and on the street and then things start to come together.

F \ Are there any differences between creating patterns for house ware and fashion? Which is more exciting to you?
H \ Not really when it comes to looks and ideas. But with wallpapers and ceramics you have to be more precise with your artwork. If the pattern doesn't join well – you will see it! Prints for fashion fold and follow the body and you will not see "mistakes" easily. Both are just exiting.

F \ How do you define your design style? Do you always want it to be colorful, optimistic and elegant?
H \ For me design is all about great ideas and smart solutions with a visual attraction that makes people look and think. Whatever the project and client is it will need a creative solution and that does not need to have a set style. However today I work a lot with prints and patterns. These are often illustrative and may not have a set idea; they are often more build on intuition. So here I contradict myself and maybe the contradiction and intuition is my own "style". I sometimes see my work process and prints similar to a DJ or a musician. I work with different rhythms that I combine in a big collage, a collage that reflect the world I live in today, which to me is like a big patchwork of different cultures and visual expressions.

F \ What was the life like when you were a student at St. Martins College in London? What made you move back to Stockholm?
H \ St Martins showed to be very good for me, it really opened up my way of thinking and made me start questioning why I made certain choices in my design. I also think I got really influenced by my time in London because it has such a mixture of different cultures and nationalities. That made me very curious and made me look at things in new directions. I never planned to stay in London but lived there for another three years after college working at Foundation 33. However I always knew I should go back to Sweden, that's where home is.

Laurent Desgrange \ France

Laurent Desgrange was born in Paris in 1982 and spent the majority of his childhood in Tahiti, French Polynesia.

His work is a mix of historical figures, popular icons and images twisted in a classical spirit but yet with a modern graphic touch. He can create a fantasized reality ruled by a logic of his own. Recalling images from his childhood or his fantasy, Laurent Desgrange's illustrations depict archetypes and characters from a mythology of his own. Portraying these characters with a joyous sense of reality, his extremely subtle, impeccably beautiful images serve as metaphors for earlier more innocent times while simultaneously commenting on current society of much movement, violence and even humor.

F \ How do you describe Laurent Desgrange's personality?
L \ Skilful hands, oriented ideas.

F \ What was the idea behind Laurent Desgrange's T-shirts?
L \ Not an idea, a bodily form. A cool and easy way to showcase my aesthetics!

F \ What made Laurent Desgrange standout and won Who's Next Fashion Designer Contest in 2007?
L \ The universe was ready!

F \ Laurent Desgrange's illustration is always impeccable. Where the inspiration comes from?
L \ Lady Oscar, sci-fi mythology, Rondo Veneziano & my cactus lounge at home.

F \ Was Laurent Desgrange trained to be a fashion designer or born to be a fashion artist?
L \ "The happy medium, here's the wisdom. » Confucius.

F \ What did Laurent Desgrange want to be when he was a little boy?
L \ One colorful and vibrant Tahitian pareo.

5PREVIEW \ Italy

5PREVIEW was created by coincidence in January 2008. Emeli Martensson, the designer behind the brand, makes simple white T-shirts with bold black prints, high quality cotton, tailored in Italy, and hand printed, playing with famous logos like Chanel, Marc Jacobs, Collosseum, Tour Eiffel; dirty handwritings like "Stop Making Sense" and "C'est la vie".

Having a background of graphic design, fashion design, drawing, industrial design, interior design and sociology, the 360°creative person Emeli gets her admirers who are fashionistas, punks, spoiled teenagers, moms in their 30ies, hipsters, artists and musicians, unisex.

F \ Why did you take 5PREVIEW as your brand name? What does it stand for?

E \ As all good things it just came to my mind without thinking too much. To name a brand is really difficult so you had better not think too much and not make to conceptual stuff with too many thoughts behind. "Preview" because I wanted to see the T-shirt collection as a preview for something bigger, a small collection with unisex clothes, and to be exact, a 5-piece collection, that is why I used the number five.

F \ You worked for a big Italian brand for several years before setting up 5PREVIEW. What did you do in the Italian brand company, and how did it affect your later development?

E \ I worked as a print designer, doing mostly allover prints. The target was teenage girls so I worked as an illustrator putting my drawings on fabrics. It was great because I had a lot of creative freedom but in the end with the economical crisis this brand was saving a bit too much money cutting down on the quality, cutting down on everything. So I thought it was time to leave the ship after more than 4 years there. I learned a lot about the fashion business there, such as how to create a commercial collection and how less important the creative part of the process is than the commercial part with promoting and such.

F \ Besides T-shirts, you have started a jewellery line as cool as usual. What do you enjoy the most during the design process?

E \ I love the results. I love photo shooting. I love touching that plexiglas pendant that came out so good. I love working with the visual presentation of the brand. I love working as an art-director for a project. I love people that are helping me out with the practical stuff. I love when I can't fall asleep because I got my head filled with ideas.

F \ Do you have any plan to enlarge your business while still keeping it stylish?

E \ Yes, that is the idea. The only problem is that people love printed stuff, it's like they're buying an image, but in the clothes collection I don't want to put prints. So I have to re-interpret the printed T-shirts into simple basic wearable clothes (concentrating on high quality materials and clean cuts). It's less commercial and therefore a real challenge.

F \ Do you have any fashion designers that you really look up to? And what have you learnt from those designers?

E \ I look up to people like Swedish Örjan Andersson, head designer and founder of the jeansbrand Cheap Monday because he started out without a big budget creating a world known brand from nothing! There must be a lot of hard work. I've learned that the crowd wants wearable stuff. You see people graduated from fashion schools making unbearable pieces of art but that's not fashion design for me. Usually the best thing is just to simplify a bit. As one of the prints in my last collection says "Less Is More".

NDEUR \ France

The NDEUR shoe concept was born in May 2007. Mathieu Missiaen, the designer behind the brand, decorates leather pumps with unique designs and patterns handcrafted from oil-based paints. Although there are standard designs to his work, each pair is uniquely one of a kind as they are handmade. NDEUR shoes can be viewed as serving a dual purpose as not only a fashion statement but a work of art.

NDEUR's online shoe sales along with retail points of sale have shown substantial international demand and growth ranging from the US, UK, Spain, France, Belgium, Australia , Brazil, Japan, Kuwait , etc.

F \ How long have you been painting shoes? How many pairs of shoes have been painted by you?
N \ I start painting shoes almost 3 years ago and I might have done around 300 pairs so far.

F \ What makes you so fascinated in painting?
N \ I don't know. I used to paint on canvas. I guess painting high-heels offers me the possibility to have a new medium to express myself, a little bit like a sketch book. Because I had so much order last year that I didn't had time to do research. Basically my research was directly on the shoes.

F \ What type of designer are you? Who do you think would be your buyers?
N \ I get bored very fast so I have to change my support as soon as possible. I love to change my style as well and I really don't want to have just one style. I want to be able to express myself without an unmovable style.
I guess my buyers are young, love the art-graphic world, the new media, and the new way to express.

F \ Any competitors so far? Who do you think is your biggest competition?
N \ Myself. I am never happy with what I finished.

F \ What has been the best for you?
N \ My collaboration with Microsoft and Fiat, some picture of my shoe in the Vans history book.

F \ What does your label Ndeur stand for?
N \ Evolution and always push a little bit further my art and all my ideas.

Dismissed \ Spain

Dismissed was born in March 2008, when the designer Alba Brito Beaujon (Barcelona, 1982) began to experiment with serigraphy. She wanted to do something with great visual impact, so T-shirts and tote bags would be the perfect canvas for her project. Attracted by all kinds of symbolism, the referents for her collection are clearly influenced by advertising. The impact she was searching for was to take symbols and icons which are clearly stuck to a value. What symbolically can't fit, like haute couture and chicken wings, graphically make a double sense. It all comes back to mixing opposite graphic elements to reveal a reality dominated by a huge ad campaign.

F \ What is your fashion background?
D \ I studied fashion design in Bau Design School (Barcelona), where I revealed what really thrills me: Fashion and visual communication.
I finished my studies in 2005 and since then I've worked as a freelance designer for a few different companies making collaborations for their collections. Lately I've done some works as an advertising stylist, but this work was the less creative of all. It was in 2007 when I rent a studio with a friend and we started to create new projects, each one by our side; and since then I've been working on my own stuff.

F \ Where did you draw inspiration from for your logo design? Why is it special?
D \ Dismissed was the name of a project I made at the university consisting in a collection based exclusively by the results of psycho technical tests made for people who had been fired of their jobs, the points of the test that were "not correct" were the characteristics I considered most valuable for starting to design. I really enjoyed this project because I've always felt special attraction to the other side of success, the mediocre and shabby side so charming and so ignored for all. Then I took the hospital cross shape in black, I liked the result.

F \ What style would you classify your line as?
D \ In this collection I think people use the t-shirts like a claim. It is not necessary to be a fashion expert to know who is the man of the white ponytail or the editor-in-chief of the most influential fashion magazine worldwide; people who wear this collection are fans of advertising and visual communication.

F \ What do you think makes the collection stand out?
D \ I think that decontextualization in any aspect is very attractive when it creates a great visual impact.

F \ Did anyone help when you set up your label?
D \ I like to take care of everything when I start a new project. Obviously I've worked with some professional photographers who had helped me a lot to go ahead.

F \ You have made some strong graphic tees so far. Would you do more change on the print or start some other new line in the future?
D \ Yes, I will start a new line in the future, but what's going to be changed is the support. I will keep working on graphic elements over the garments but this time with other patterns, not just T-shirts.

Uniforms for the
Dedicated \ Sweden

Uniforms for the Dedicated is put forth by creators with various creative backgrounds and ideas. The label serves as a platform for musicians, illustrators, designers, and more, thus creating a collective force of a widespread creative network. Based on diverse talent, Uniforms produce and distribute men's fashion and music in combination with art and film.

Uniforms for the Dedicated was awarded "Upcoming brand of the year 2008" by the Swedish Fashion Council during Stockholm Fashion Week.

F \ What was the story behind Uniforms for the Dedicated?
U \ The primary purpose of Uniforms has never been merely fashion. Instead the foundation of what we are today took form years ago - a group of friends travelling the world snowboarding. Later we realized we wanted to continue the creative journey together and fashion became the tool we gathered around. It allowed us to apply and combine various expressions such as art, design, and music. Sure we had no previous experience in clothing design or production at start (yeah it's been a long ride) but in the long run I believe the incentives and diverse backgrounds of ours work to our favor.

F \ Does Uniforms for the Dedicated have strict requirements for the style?
U \ Although it may seem like creative anarchy it's not the complete truth. Everything we do co-play with a greater purpose. Each step or new partnership is a result of a shared vision. Our clothing design is one example. At least we tend to have an idea of what we like to accomplish. The journey however is more of a roller coaster.
It's rarely a one man's job although each participating creator may be given the free role after the objectives have been set together. However, few things are finally lunched without being collectively tested and argued. It's a fun and challenging process. It should be looked as an opportunity to progress.

F \ What is the story about the SS09 illustrations?
U \ The SS09 illustrations tell the story how music shapes environments. As a result the illustrations are oceans of various motions and emotions.

F \ Do you have stockist anywhere in the world?
U \ Uniforms for the Dedicated is sold in following locations among others; Solo, Grandpa and PUB (Uniforms concept store) Stockholm, Fever Gothenburg, Tjallamalla Malmö, Pede & Stoffer and Illum Copenhagen, Behave London, Hip-store Leeds, Autograph Birmingham, Wood Wood Berlin, Urban Outfitters Hamburg, Kiliwatch Paris, Concrete Amsterdam, Freudian Kicks Oslo, Beamhill Helsinki, Addicted Seoul, Macondo Verona. In total 80 stores around the world.

F \ What has been the best for you so far? And what would be your next step?
U \ It's been a long journey of learning by doing so far. Many different things; a good party somewhere, words from someone you really respect saying "hey guys great stuff", the office space we have come across, first pay check, everything we learned and people met, and so on. Honestly we wouldn't be much without all mistakes we've made.
Apart from new markets, we'll keep develop the ways we make our design and music, look into new markets such as Japan and U.S., and start looking into new product categories. Uniforms as a creative agency...

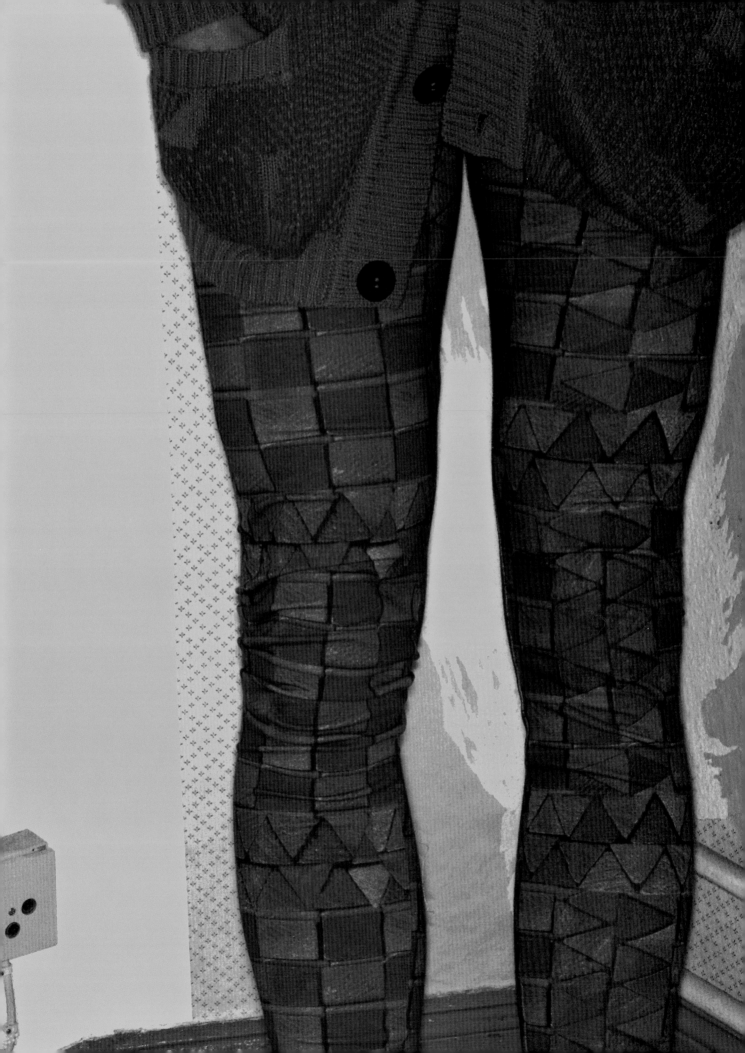

AUTUMN

My homeland is like an eternal autumn, a bit
beautifully sad, melancholic, tenderly tiny-rainy,
sophisticated dark and epic silent. It has depths
with everfrost, base ground that never melts before
the new ice arrives.

Taigas are like a secret, wise and self-conscious
calm. Trees stand with their soothing permanence.
They stay, how ever painful will autumn cause,
strong to fight for season change. You can scent and
see the different tone, when the longing autumn
wind hits the deep green wilder fields.

Autumn that needs to end, permanently falling
asleep before something new can be born. That's a
rule for creativity. That´s a rule for living clean deep.

—Paola Ivana Suhonen

I tryed to dance you out of my head

TITLE: The Land of Dreams \ **FASHION**: Kling by Kling \ **GRAPHIC**: Kling by Kling \ **PHOTO**: Studio SEEK
STYLING: Kling \ **MAKE-UP**: Kling \ **MODEL**: Fredrik \ **YEAR**: 2008
DESCRIPTION: The collection is built on different characters all taken from Kling's own daydreams, given different names. The patterns is then built around the characters and given life through the shapes of the garment. This collection is a place between dreams and reality with styles that bring the thoughts to Japan street culture at the same time elegance, craziness, and fantasy. All to highlight the feeling of getting surrounded of the patterns and actually make you feel like you inside the land of dreams...

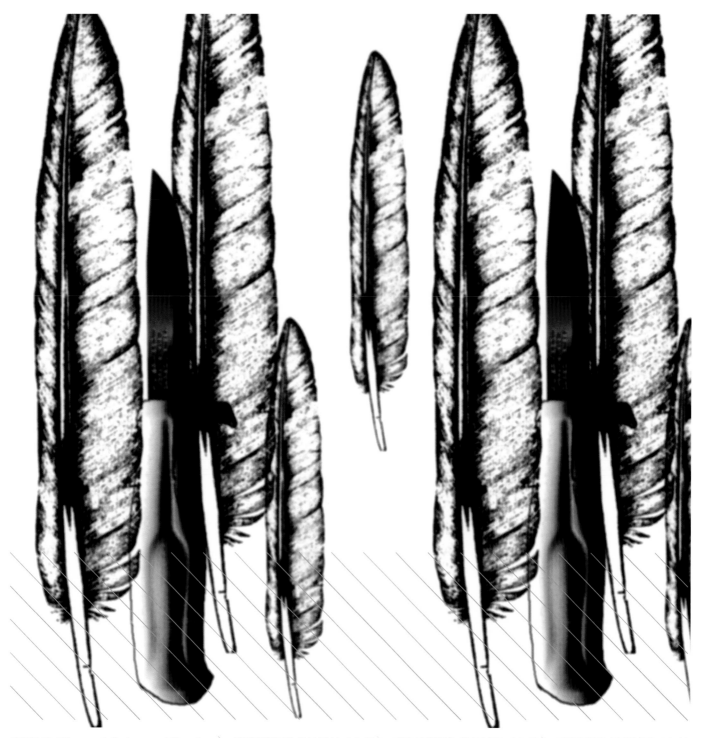

TITLE: Diamond, Stripes and Revolver \ **FASHION**: IVANAhelsinki \ **GRAPHIC**: IVANAhelsinki \ **PHOTO**: IVANAhelsinki

DESCRIPTION: "Many years ago, one deadcalm beautiful day, at noon. I met the love of my life. He arrived none too soon. He was called Jack Diamond and he looked like Jack White, from White Stripes. Black beard lichen hair to his shoulders, sweetdirty words, evil smile and warlock greeneyes. He wore clean white spats with tailored black suite and I thought he might be a leftover preerie soldier or homeless cowboy.

He drowned me into the flood of love. He said I looked like a lost and found Bambi. He said I was his Bambi. And he also said, we were coming from the same northern unknown forests, from the same mystic forgotten wild mindwoods. He told me, I was lost but he would take me home.

He was a truly dark love knight and taiga-desert rider. He was a rowdy romantic and his time was ruthlessly running the wrong way. He was second from God. He was hardly none.

And I loved him. More than anything. I loved him until one day again, he shot me to death. With his iron revolver. And wounded I was. And finally dead."

Abbreviated from a slavic legend, northern love story called " The diamond-eyed Bambi and his dark revolver lover."

TITLE: Hairy Shirt \ **FASHION:** Frederique Daubal \ **GRAPHIC:** Frederique Daubal \ **PHOTO:** Johanna Salomez
STYLING: Frederique Daubal \ **YEAR:** 2008
DESCRIPTION: Handmade silkscreen by Severine.

TITLE: Tokyo Camouflage \ **FASHION**: FouR \ **GRAPHIC**: Przemek Sobocki \ **PHOTO**: Pi, Maciej Kucia
STYLING: przem.ko \ **MODEL**: Kouta, Shingo Yasuda \ **YEAR**: 2008
DESCRIPTION: skulls, parts of air con in the collection.

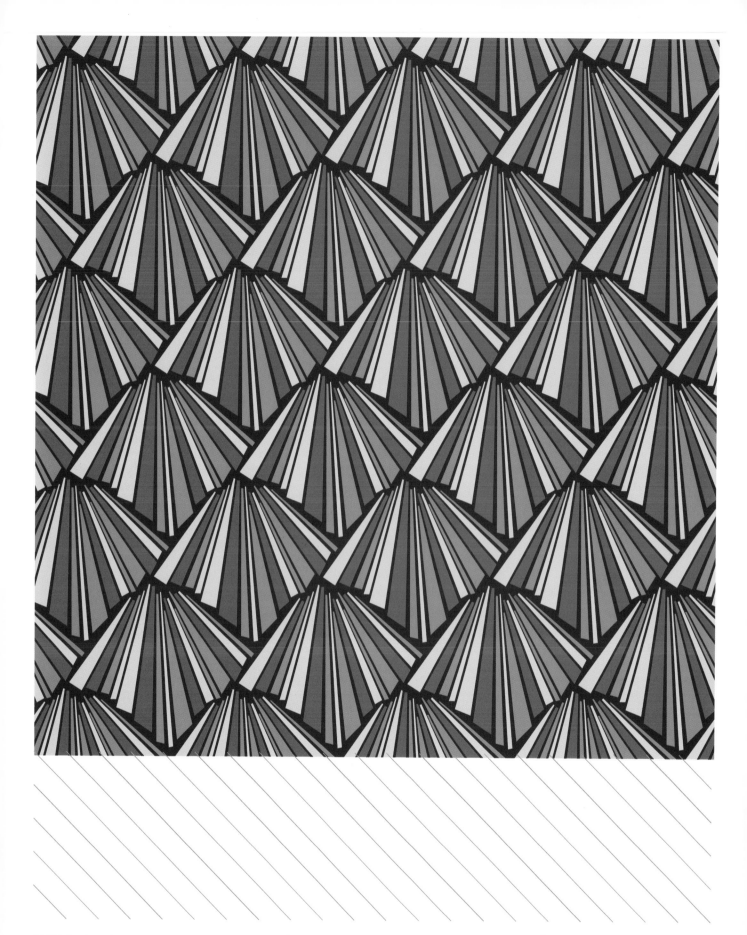

TITLE: Cape \ **FASHION:** House of Dagmar \ **GRAPHIC:** Hanna Werning \ **PHOTO:** House of Dagmar \ **YEAR:** 2007
DESCRIPTION: Inspired by the Art Deco period and the shape of a cape unfolding in the wind.

TITLE: Salmiak \ **FASHION**: House of Dagmar \ **GRAPHIC**: Hanna Werning \ **PHOTO**: House of Dagmar \ **YEAR**: 2006
DESCRIPTION: Inspired by the Art Deco period.

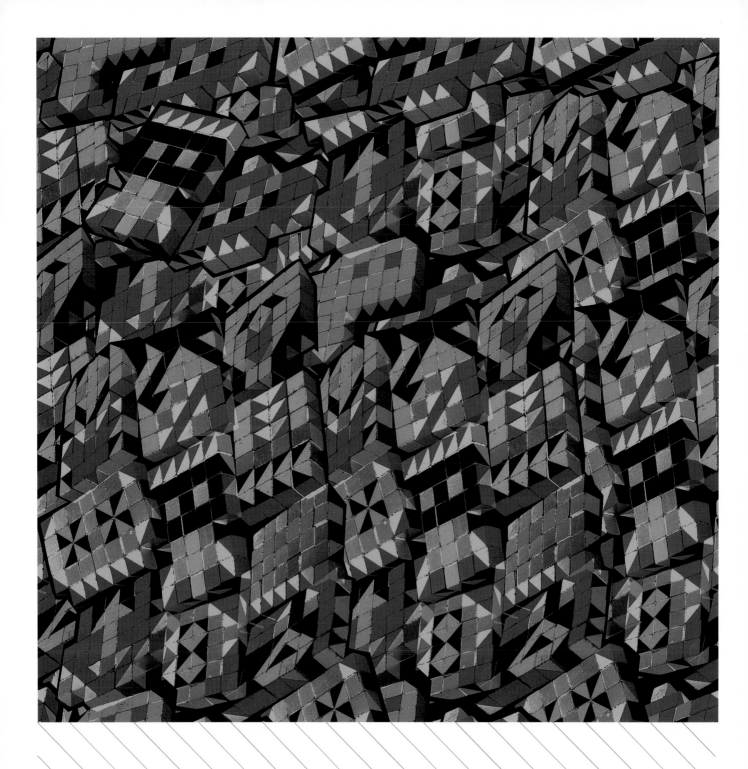

TITLE: Totem Collection \ **FASHION**: potipoti \ **GRAPHIC**: Nando Cornejo & Silvia Salvador \ **PHOTO**: Frank Kalero
STYLING: Silvia S. Kopp \ **MODEL**: Irene \ **YEAR**: 2008
DESCRIPTION: A set of designs inspired in Native Americans Totems of polychromatic wood as well as on vintage wooden toys. Beige, black, navy blue and colorful prints are the signature of this collection.

FASHION: Sandor Lakatos   **PHOTO**: Tamas Dobos   **STYLING**: Kata Florian & Judy Judas   **HAIR**: Robert Radinkovics
MAKE-UP: Csilla Kiss   **MODEL**: Jani   **YEAR**: 2008

TITLE: Berlin Closer Collection \ **FASHION**: potipoti \ **GRAPHIC**: Nando Cornejo & Silvia Salvador \ **PHOTO**: potipoti
YEAR: 2009
DESCRIPTION: The collection name "Berlin Closer" evolved from the titles of the music albums "Berlin" by Lou Reed and "Closer" by Joy Division and stands for the intense connection of Silvia and Nando to the city.
Expressive graphic-prints, inspired by triangular retro-building bricks, which Silvia and Nando are collecting since many years, are the main theme of the new potipoti-collection.

TITLE: Berlin Closer Collection \ **FASHION**: potipoti \ **GRAPHIC**: Nando Cornejo & Silvia Salvador
PHOTO: Frank Kalero \ **STYLING**: Reiner Metz \ **HAIR**: Natty Grier \ **MAKE-UP**: Natty Grier
MODEL: Conrad (izaio models) \ **YEAR**: 2009
DESCRIPTION: Expressive graphic-prints, inspired by triangular retro-building bricks, which Silvia and Nando are collecting
since many years, are the main theme of the new potipoti-collection.

TITLE: Berlin Closer Collection \ **FASHION:** potipoti \ **GRAPHIC:** Nando Cornejo & Silvia Salvador
PHOTO: Frank Kalero \ **STYLING:** Jorge Olmedo \ **HAIR:** Loreal \ **MAKE-UP:** Loreal \ **MODEL:** Fon \ **YEAR:** 2009
DESCRIPTION: Fashion show at Madrid Fashion Week.

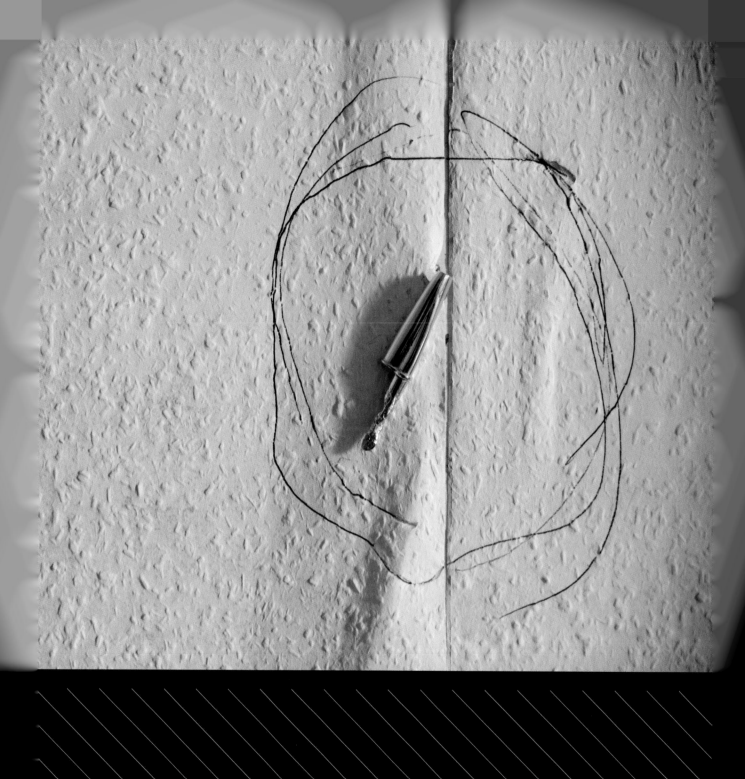

TITLE: Bik, Silver Silence, Bik, Gummi of the collection 'Things That Might As Well Be...' \ **DESIGN**: Martine Viergever
PHOTO: Thomas Voorn \ **STYLING**: Thomas Voorn \ **MODEL**: Marije \ **YEAR**: 2007
DESCRIPTION: Ordinary objects from kitchen drawers and dusty corners are dug up by the designer in order to elevate them to the status of jewel. The shape remains unchanged; the function of the object is simply shifted to a place of honour: hung around the neck or pinned on the chest.

TITLE: Strap, Wristwallet of the collection 'Season's Greetings' \ **DESIGN**: Martine Viergever \ **PHOTO**: Thomas Voorn
STYLING: Thomas Voorn \ **MODEL**: Matthijs \ **YEAR**: 2008
DESCRIPTION: 'Season's Greetings' to the designer developed as a very nostalgic collection which led her back to the days when she had to bike 15 miles to school through stormy autumn weather. "Strap" is a multifunctional jewellery piece and is commonly

TITLE: Totem Collection **FASHION**: potipoti **GRAPHIC**: Nando Cornejo & Silvia Salvador **PHOTO**: Frank Kalero
STYLING: Silvia S. Kopp **MODEL**: Irene **YEAR**: 2008
DESCRIPTION: There is always a bit of a fable in potipoti's designs. Totem, there is a pinch of folklore and a lot of imagination.
The use of graphics and the shape of garments improve in each season. They bring from icy Berlin this their fifth and most grown
up to date collection, a very colorful set of designs inspired in Native Americans Totems of polychromatic wood as well as on
vintage wooden toys. Beige, black, navy blue and colorful prints are the signature of this collection.

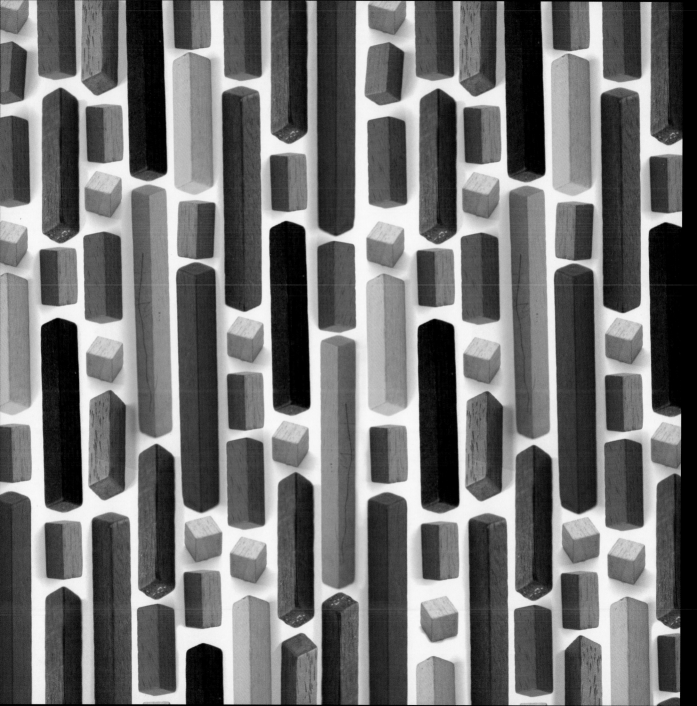

TITLE: Mod. Preview \ **GRAPHIC:** 5PREVIEW \ **PHOTO:** Giorgia Placidi \ **STYLING:** Emelie Martensson \
MODEL: Greta \ **YEAR:** 2009 \
DESCRIPTION: White T-shirt & white cotton tote bag mod. Preview from the THIRD COLLECTION

TITLE: Bestiario Collection \ **FASHION**: potipoti \ **GRAPHIC**: Nando Cornejo & Silvia Salvador
PHOTO: Nando Cornejo \ **YEAR**: 2007
DESCRIPTION: Scary monsters uhhhhh!

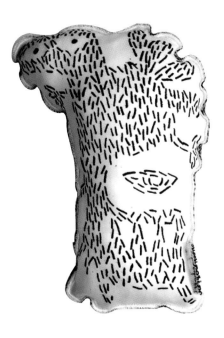

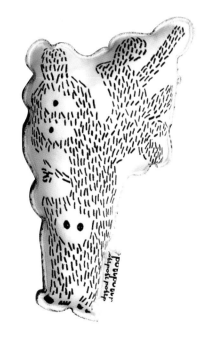

TITLE: The Land of Dreams ＼ **FASHION**: Kling by Kling ＼ **GRAPHIC**: Kling by Kling ＼ **PHOTO**: Studio SEEK
STYLING: Kling ＼ **MAKE-UP**: Kling ＼ **MODEL**: Fredrik ＼ **YEAR**: 2008
DESCRIPTION: The collection is built on different characters all taken from Kling's own daydreams, given different names. The patterns is then built around the characters and given life through the shapes of the garment. This collection is a place between dreams and reality with styles that bring the thoughts to Japan street culture at the same time elegance, craziness, and fantasy. All to highlight the feeling of getting surrounded of the patterns and actually make you feel like you inside the land of dreams...

TITLE: Mod. Y5L and PREVIEW by 5preview for WEEKDAY \ **GRAPHIC**: 5PREVIEW for WEEKDAY
MODEL: Carolina & Andreas \ **YEAR**: 2009
DESCRIPTION: Shirts from the collaboration 5preview for WEEKDAY, watercolor & ink illustration by Emeli

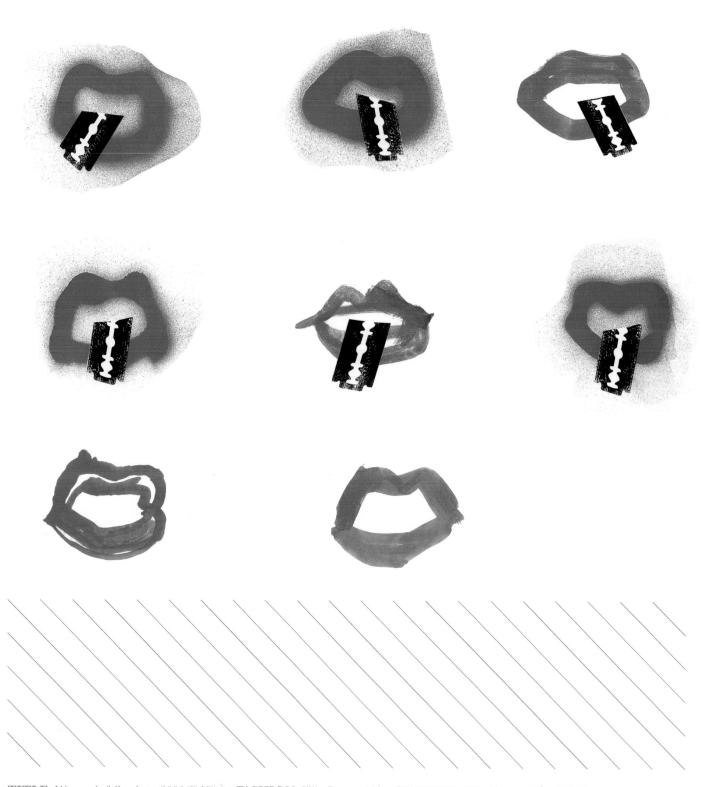

TITLE: Women's fall_winter2000(CdG) ＼ **FASHION**: Filip Pagowski ＼ **GRAPHIC**: Filip Pagowski ＼ **YEAR**: 2000

TITLE: Bits, Web, Web, It's raining cats & dogs of the collection 'Season's Greetings' \ **DESIGN**: Martine Viergever
PHOTO: Thomas Voorn \ **STYLING**: Thomas Voorn \ **MODEL**: Katinka, Matthijs \ **YEAR**: 2008
DESCRIPTION: The nostalgia in 'Season's Greetings' continues by the pieces "Web" and "It's raining cats & dogs". The designer used to make tinkering with forest fruits, sate sticks and matches in kindergarten. Even the sate sticks and matches are executed in silver.

FASHION: Sandor Lakatos   PHOTO: Tamas Dobos   STYLING: Kata Florian & Judy Judas   HAIR: Robert Radinkovics
MAKE-UP: Csilla Kiss   MODEL: Jam   YEAR: 2008

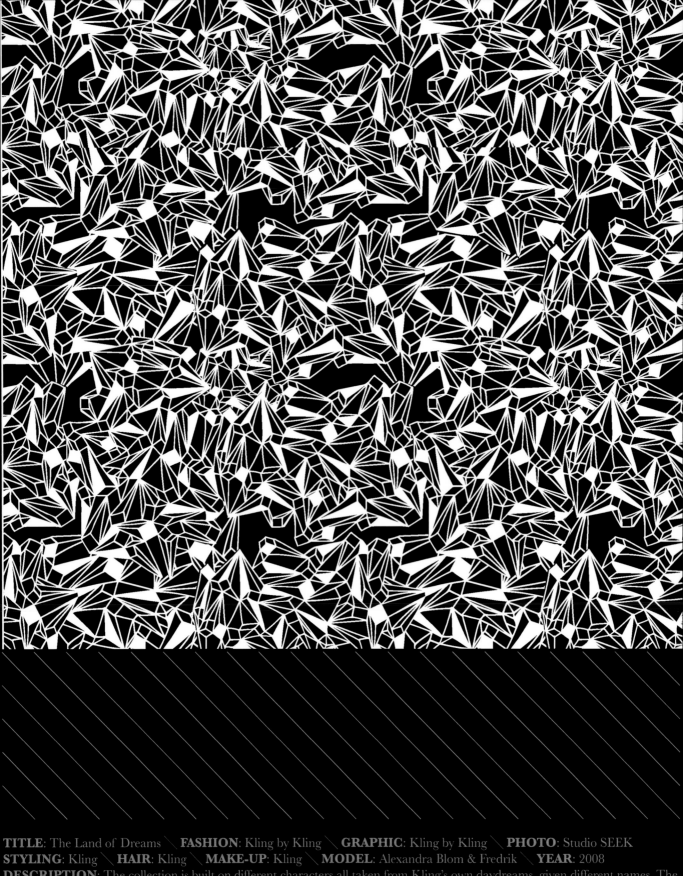

TITLE: The Land of Dreams \ **FASHION**: Kling by Kling \ **GRAPHIC**: Kling by Kling \ **PHOTO**: Studio SEEK
STYLING: Kling \ **HAIR**: Kling \ **MAKE-UP**: Kling \ **MODEL**: Alexandra Blom & Fredrik \ **YEAR**: 2008
DESCRIPTION: The collection is built on different characters all taken from Kling's own daydreams, given different names. The patterns is then built around the characters and given life through the shapes of the garment. This collection is a place between dreams and reality with styles that bring the thoughts to Japan street culture at the same time elegance, craziness, and fantasy. All to highlight the feeling of getting surrounded of the patterns and actually make you feel like you inside the land of dreams...

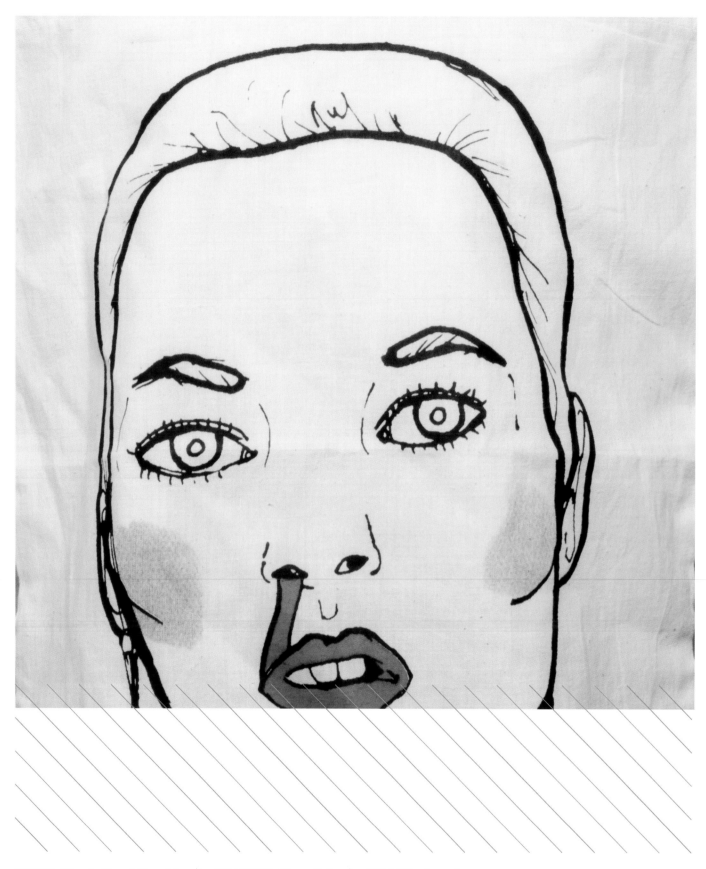

TITLE: Bloody Nosed Kate Moss \ **GRAPHIC**: Elena Gallen \ **PHOTO**: Cesar Segarra
STYLING: Raquel Galvan, Elena Gallen \ **MAKEUP**: Raquel Galvan \ **MODEL**: Raquel Galvan \ **YEAR**: 2008
DESCRIPTION: Irony and minimalism in huge colorful screen printed basic white t-shirts. Illustrations of bloody nosed Kate Moss, Paris Hilton's chihuahua Tinkerbelle and the collaboration with rock star Wendy James in a unique tour t-shirt. This collection includes a natural colored tote bag with Kate Moss' illustration, which has by now become a postmodern icon.

TITLE: Double-headed Bambis \ **GRAPHIC**: Elena Gallen \ **PHOTO**: Cesar Segarra
STYLING: Raquel Galvan, Elena Gallen \ **MAKEUP**: Raquel Galvan \ **MODEL**: Raquel Galvan \ **YEAR**: 2007
DESCRIPTION: A series of illustrations based on the concept of hibrytation. With opposite essences, the ideal world of fantasy and the cruel world of rarities/malformations will be eternally addressed to different targets, the children and the adult, but will equally become grotesque and profitable. These illustrations play with the well-known icons of Disney's fairy-tales converting them into circus freaks.

THE BEAUTY ISSUE

TITLE: Vogue Can \ **GRAPHIC**: Alba Brito for Dismissed \ **PHOTO**: Ivan Llamas \ **STYLING**: Alba Brito
MAKE-UP: Erica Mann \ **MODEL**: Barbara Masiá \ **YEAR**: 2008
DESCRIPTION: Seven top models of the decade photographied by Meisel. Best hairstyle, best makeup, best post-production. The most beautiful faces are the cover of one of the most. The picture was on the cover of one of the well-known fashion magazines in the world.

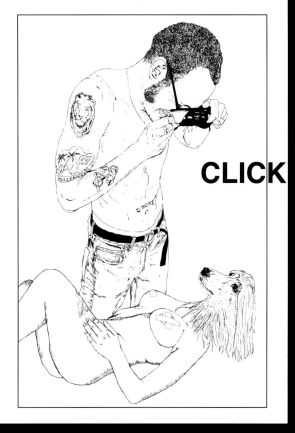

CLICK

FASHION: Cooperative Designs \ **GRAPHIC**: Cooperative Designs \ **PHOTO**: Roger Dean
STYLING: Elizabeth Cardwell \ **YEAR**: 2009
DESCRIPTION: Gracie Cardigan, Gracie Dress; Lycra and Wool striped jumper and trousers, matching scarf. Inspired by a friend, photographer and muse Amy Gwatkin. The collection captured a sense of English eccentricity within the collection, mixing traditional winter knits with graphic patterns in a strict color palette. Materials were experimental, combining lycra with wools to create textured fantasy knits.

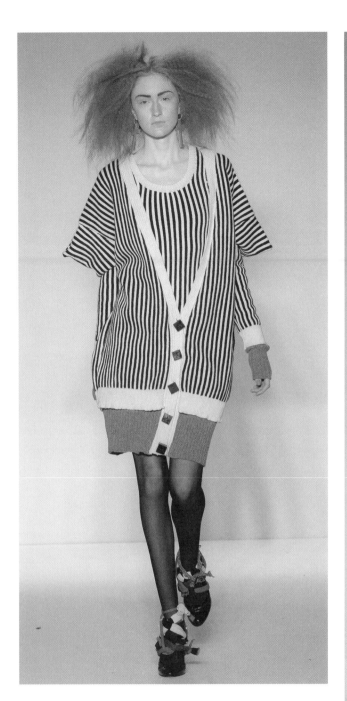

TITLE: Heavy Bag ＼ **DESIGN**: Hoiming Fung & Baldwin Pui ＼ **PHOTO**: Jacky Chee ＼ **YEAR**: 2006
DESCRIPTION: "Funny Horror" chain-ball bag. The "58kg" means special to the designer because she was told by a doctor that it should be her "standard weight" according to her height...and it was how she felt about the recommendation.

INTERVIEW

Elena Gallen \ Spain

Elena Gallen (born 1984) is a freelance artist based in Barcelona. Graduated from college in Media Studies in Barcelona and filmmaking studies at the New York Film Academy (Hollywood), Elena has experienced in fashion design (prints and illustration) and is specially known for her collection of t-shirts that quickly garnered a cult-following among the Fashion Elite.
Combining naive, odd and minimalistic, and inspired by trash culture, cult movies, postmodernism, consumerism and an unusual taste for monsters, UFO, blush, red lipstick, ligers, galaxies, horror films, transgression, teenagers and nature, the character embodied by the artist has beyond her creations.

F \ It is very lovely that when you were a child you dressed up as Alaska in kindergarden. You were born to be a fashion addict, weren't you?
E \ Not really. As an only child I found that dressing up is a single and creative game I loved to play. As growing up I didn't lose that sense of joy and self-expression with clothing. Obviously, I became aware of tendencies but I always liked staying ahead of mainstream fashion. Sometimes I find myself more in the mood for Japanese costume role-playing than reading VOGUE.

F \ You love luxury as much as you love trash, that's why you like to define your style as glamour-trash art. What do you see the connection between luxury and trash?
E \ I used to define my style in those terms when I started illustrating popular icons with a twist of irony and horror. I think both concepts are complementary. Luxury and trash are two sides of the same coin. Stripping settled aesthetic icons of their essence makes such a deep impact in viewers. It's the combination of apparently opposites that's unexpected.

F \ What is your design formula?
E \ The time cycles in fashion are shockingly fast these days. So designing something brilliant isn't necessarily linked to succeeding. I guess my design formula was to create something fresh and commercialized at the right time.

F \ What is the story behind your white tees?
E \ I printed simple and iconic illustrations in basic t-shirts because it was aesthetically calm and attractive for my own eyes. In that time of overdose I happened to appear as a pioneer of t-shirt minimalism. The basic white t-shirts and the powerful images amused people because of how different it was to the actual trend back then.

F \ Over seven years of graphic and web design experience, will you focus more on fashion design in the future?
E \ For a long time I didn't consider myself a fashion designer but an artist whose illustrations were printed on a t-shirt. T-shirts were for me a different canvas to exhibit my creations. After two clean collections and different t-shirt designs for clients, my designs are evolving and I have come to understand the potential of a t-shirt.

F \ Which potential market have you seen and wanted to develop?
E \ I consciously didn't choose my market, it chose me. It's a mixture of trend-setters, clubbers, spoiled teenagers, artists, photographers, deejays, stylists, models and wannabes. I really like my market because it's brave, fetishistic and wealthy.

Filip Pagowski \ USA

Filip Pagowski is a graphic artist from Warsaw and New York working mostly in Asia and the US, specializing in the frontier territory cross pollination of fine art and graphic design, often resulting in illustration projects for visually challenged journalistic or fiction pieces; image, logo and print design for fashion clients; and participation in hard to define exhibition or installation projects. He spends winters skiing; freeriding in the French Alps, in and around Chamonix.

F \ You called yourself graphic artist rather than graphic designer. What are the differences?
P \ I feel like I fall in a gray area between graphics and the fine arts. My work does not strictly represent graphic design but rather the artistic fringe of that category. Most of my work is done without the use of a computer, is less structured and has an unruly, more fine art directed quality.
That's why I think graphic designer would be a slightly misleading representation of my professional character. I feel like "graphic artist" better represents my attitude and who I am.

F \ Your clients are from America to Europe to Asia. How do you manage to make your work attractive to different culture?
P \ The clients usually approach me for what I represent. They find what I do interesting and close to their sensibility. With my Polish background and other influences mixed in, I cover enough of the visual terrain to satisfy the curious and adventurous, wherever they might be.

F \ What is your personality? Do any of your attitudes reflect on your design?
P \ I'm pretty sure they must. Even though I like simple things, I feel my personality's quite complicated. Maybe part of the "problem" is that I'm a Gemini, so there is two of us....

F \ When did you find yourself interested in graphic design and how did you develop your interest?
P \ I remember as a kid, around 6 years old, watching my father (Henryk Tomaszewski) work. He designed posters. I loved observing him work and felt intrigued by the subject matter and the idea of solving a specific visual problem. At the end the job would get printed, therefore multiplied, and shown in many places at the same time. What more one would expect?

F \ What else may amuse you as much as graphic design in your life?
P \ Music, architecture, skiing, adventure, women...

F \ Which country do you always want to visit but not yet had a chance?
P \ China, Iran...

Martine Viergever \ the Netherlands

Dutch jewellery designer Martine Viergever is trained as a goldsmith at the Vakschool in Schoonhoven, the Netherlands. After completing this, she studied fashion and forecast at the Willem de Kooning Art Academy in Rotterdam, the Netherlands and graduated cum laude in 2003.

She gained working experience at Bless in Berlin, Germany. Martine Viergever launched her jewellery label in 2006. Besides designing her own jewellery collections, she also designs accessories and jewellery commissioned by several fashion brands such as Monique van Heist and Francisco van Benthum.

F \ What is your design background?
M \ After studying goldmithing, I continued studying both Collection and Forecast at the fashion department of the Willem de Kooning Art Academy in Rotterdam, the Netherlands and graduated cum laude. I worked for a while at Bless in Berlin. In 2006 I launched my first jewelry collection and since then I annually design new collections under my own label and in commission for Dutch fashion designers Monique van Heist and Francisco van Benthum, etc.

F \ How did you get started designing Jewelry?
M \ It was initially based upon the concept of a collection I did when graduating at the Fashion department at art school. Daily surrounding things are easy to be neglected, such as envelopes, telephone books, trash bags. I translated their texture into textile, their forms into silhouettes and silkscreened and prints.
Pen caps, a vent key, a bath plug. I liked their modesty, and things are the wall flowers, the underdogs, the grey mice in existence. I brought an ode to them by handcrafting in sterling silver and other precious materials such as gem stones and leather in order to elevate them to the status of jewel. These pieces grew into a constantly evolving collection of jewelry to which new items are consistently added.

F \ Your design looks conceptual rather than commercial. Would you make the pieces more from your intuition or for your clients?
M \ Fashion exists by the grace of persistent change. It can not be rigid, it has to move. As an artist I think it is my role to lead fashion into different and unexpected ways and be the one to change fashion constantly. The definition of what is esthetic is not fixed and that is what makes it interesting.
Fashion commerciality tends to slow fashion down, because that is just making a product that people already know. To me, that is too easy. And people therefore look the same without being aware of it. I have a small group of audience buying my jewelry pieces. I like that. That's how I am able to stand out with my designs.

F \ Are there any persons having been giving you great support on your creative journey that you feel grateful for?
M \ Yes! I get great support at home from my partner who knows how to get me to the essence of my work. My dear inspiring friend Thomas Voorn has the talent to show me a different point of view in just one word, just after I thought I approached something from all angles.
Thomas does both the photography and styling for my collections and we will be building installations with my jewelry in shops.

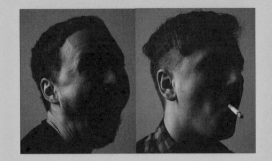

CHICKENSHIT \ Russia

The idea of CHICKENSHIT was born in 2006. Three persons (DJ, designer and photographer) did graphic designs, photos, and videos, organized parties under the name of CHICKENSHIT.
The first collection of clothes was launched in 2008 and it consisted of t-shirts dedicated to famous fashion designers.
At the moment CHICKENSHIT is working on the collection dedicated to religion and searching for the place to organize the next exhibition with Finish photographer Diana Luganski.

F \ Why did you take your brand name CHICKENSHIT?
C \ We just like how it sounds! Just slang!

F \ The label was originally created non-for-profit. What made CHICKENSHIT come into being?
C \ Success made CHICKENSHIT come into being. The first store that started to work with us is one of the expensive stores in Saint Petersburg. Non-for-profit is about installations, exhibitions and parties that we organized. We made it in order to introduce to people with the new, fashion artists, and fresh tendencies.

F \ Now CHICKENSHIT is available for international wholesale. What does it take to become worldwide popular?
C \ It is our collaborations! We work with different photographers, artists, designers from all over the world.

F \ CHICKENSHIT collections are constructed in a process where creative graphics, strong concept and dark mood are the main inspiration. What is the story behind strong concept and dark mood?
C \ We pay much attention to presenting our product, which is about packaging, photographers who take the photo shoot and models that are in the advertisement. We say "no" to nice sweet boys! We claim outlaws to be the new trend in the world of fashion.

F \ What was your big move in 2008?
C \ In October 2008 fashion label CHICKENSHIT launched a project under the name "Favorite Scandinavian photographers". The first artist of this project was KNOTAN - one of the most famous and fashionable photographers from Sweden. CHICKENSHIT organized his personal exhibition in Saint Petersburg where KNOTAN represented 52 photos and in collaboration with the project, a new series of designs "CHICKENSHIT by KNOTAN" was launched.

F \ What do you hope to accomplish in the future?
C \ More exhibitions and installations! New collaborations!

KLING by KLING \ UK

KLING by KLING is a label created by London based Swede Karolina Kling. Since establishing the brand in 2006 the label has acclaimed international attention for its distinct prints and playful designs and has been described as Viktor & Rolf on acid. For the last two years she has reached a growing audience with her fourth collection, distributing worldwide.

With a background in Graphic Design, Karolina Kling, the deisnger behind the lable, has a unique take on fashion, both highly personal and yet commercial. The concept for each collection always consists of several layers; the patterns are always beautiful, but with more to them than what meet the eye.

F \ You are originally from Sweden. But your label KLING by KLING is based in London. Why is London, but not Rome, Paris or New York?

K \ I have always find London like an really inspiring place to be, and a surrounding that always move forward, twisting and shaping the styles and trends in an interesting way. And it's close to home but so different from Sweden. So I try to go a lot back and forth to get the best from both worlds.

F \ Since 2006 the label has acclaimed international attention for its distinct prints and playful designs and has been described as Viktor & Rolf on acid. How do you feel about that?

K \ Of course I find it amazing that people around me and around the world like what I do so much and that what makes me motivated to keep going forward. I just wish that I had more contact with the people buying my cloths. It's easy to just sit in the studio and work all the time.

F \ Who is your target audience?

K \ When I'm designing I'm looking inside rather than designing for the buyer. This is quite difficult as you want it to sell at the same time as being really personal. But what I learned by now is that if I do things that really like myself, so do other people. So target audience would be anyone with the same taste as mine, I guess.

F \ What kind of clothes do you usually wear? Is it very different from what you design?

K \ It changes all the time. Some periods I'm wearing my cloths a lot, and other periods I dress completely different. Now I'm in love with flowery summer trousers and white shirts with hat and sandals, so not quite like my cloths.

F \ What is your personality that your friends around think about?

K \ To get this right I should get my friends to answer this question. But I think they would say that I love to create stories behind the cloths, which reflect my fascination for people's imagination. Somehow that has to do with what I am such a down to earth and realistic person, rather than dreamy, so when I create the collections, that is sort of an escape away from the problems I have in my real life.

F \ KLING has always worked with her graphics in a 3D way. Do you agree that beauty should not stay flat but touchable and wearable?

K \ This is so personal how you like to work with your creativity and personal expression. But for me it came natural to apply my patterns and graphics on products. I saw myself as a graphic designer for years, before I realize one day that I had been doing products all the time. And I really prefer this medium; I want to get my patterns out on everything from cars, carpets, clothes, plates, and it could go on forever.

WINTER

White, quiet, soft, dark, heavy, silence, waiting for warmer times, covered trees, cold rain, slipping feet; snow turns to water turns to ice, stars lightning in the windows, decorations in colors, things hiding in snow, pale skin; visible breath in the air, calm noise from walking in just fallen snow, red noses, frozen lakes, open fires; layers and layers of clothes, the wild is melting, hard ground, stiff bones inside your body, traditions and celebrations; presents, lightings in the trees and snow covered path in the woods leading into the darkness....

—Karolina Kling

TITLE: The Land of Dreams ⟍ **FASHION**: Kling by Kling ⟍ **GRAPHIC**: Kling by Kling ⟍ **PHOTO**: Studio SEEK
STYLING: Kling ⟍ **HAIR**: Kling ⟍ **MAKE-UP**: Kling ⟍ **MODEL**: Alexandra Blom & Fredrik ⟍ **YEAR**: 2008
DESCRIPTION: The collection is built on different characters all taken from Kling's own daydreams, given different names. The patterns is then built around the characters and given life through the shapes of the garment. This collection is a place between dreams and reality with styles that bring the thoughts to Japan street culture at the same time elegance, craziness, and fantasy. All to highlight the feeling of getting surrounded of the patterns and actually make you feel like you inside the land of dreams...

TITLE: Collar Scarf & Warmer \ **FASHION**: Frederique Daubal \ **GRAPHIC**: Frederique Daubal
PHOTO: Frederique Daubal \ **STYLING**: Frederique Daubal \ **MODEL**: Romain and Johanna \ **YEAR**: 2008
DESCRIPTION: The way to reuse collar and old granny aprons.

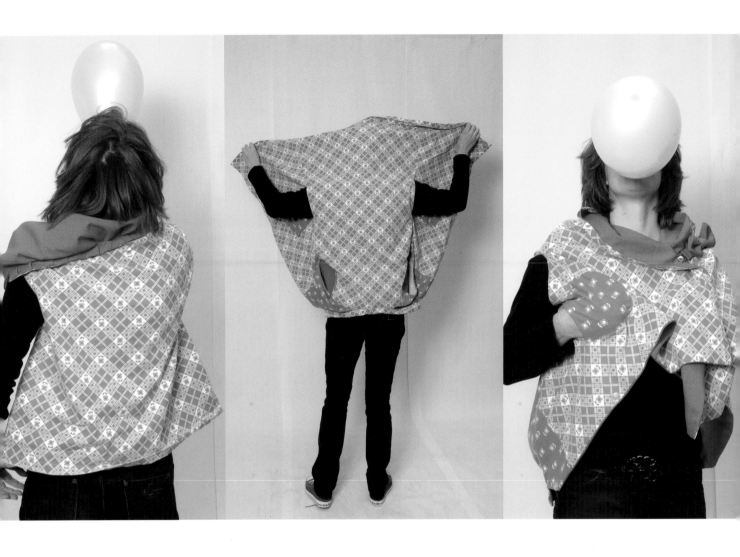

TITLE: Berlin Closer Collection \ **FASHION**: potipoti \ **GRAPHIC**: Nando Cornejo & Silvia Salvador
PHOTO: Nando Cornejo \ **YEAR**: 2009
DESCRIPTION: Expressive graphic-prints, inspired by triangular retro-building bricks, which Silvia and Nando are collecting since many years, are the main theme of the new potipoti-collection.

TITLE: Berlin Closer Collection \ **FASHION**: potipoti \ **GRAPHIC**: Nando Cornejo & Silvia Salvador
STYLING: Jorge Olmedo \ **HAIR**: Loreal \ **MAKE-UP**: Loreal \ **MODEL**: Jose Satorre \ **YEAR**: 2009
DESCRIPTION: Fashion show at Madrid Fashion Week.

TITLE: Totem Collection \ **FASHION**: potipoti   **GRAPHIC**: Nando Cornejo & Silvia Salvador   **PHOTO**: Frank Kalero
STYLING: Silvia S. Kopp \ **MODEL**: Irene \ **YEAR**: 2008
DESCRIPTION: A very colorful set of designs inspired in Native Americans Totems of polychromatic wood as well as on vintage wooden toys. Beige, black, navy blue and colorful prints are the signature of this collection.

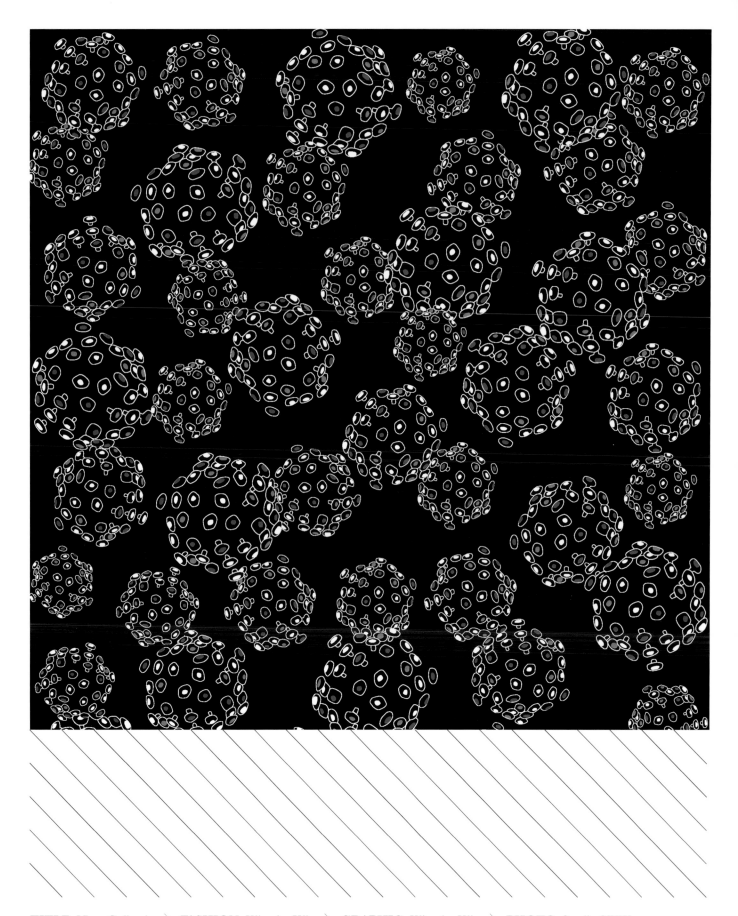

TITLE: Virus Collection \ **FASHION**: Kling by Kling \ **GRAPHIC**: Kling by Kling \ **PHOTO**: Studio SEEK
STYLING: Studio seek, Kling by Kling \ **HAIR**: Kling by Kling \ **MAKE-UP**: Kling by Kling
MODEL: Alexandra Blom and Alexander \ **YEAR**: 2007

TITLE: The Land of Dreams \ **FASHION**: Kling by Kling \ **GRAPHIC**: Kling by Kling \ **PHOTO**: Studio SEEK
STYLING: Kling \ **HAIR**: Kling \ **MAKE-UP**: Kling \ **MODEL**: Fredrik & Alexandra \ **YEAR**: 2008
DESCRIPTION: The collection is built on different characters all taken from Kling's own daydreams, given different names. The patterns is then built around the characters and given life through the shapes of the garment. This collection is a place between dreams and reality with styles that bring the thoughts to Japan street culture at the same time elegance, craziness, and fantasy. All to highlight the feeling of getting surrounded of the patterns and actually make you feel like you inside the land of dreams...

TITLE: I Want to Believe \ **ART DIRECTION**: Daniel Palillo \ **FASHION**: Daniel Palillo
GRAPHIC: Laura Laine, Daniel Palillo \ **PHOTO**: Paavo Lehtonen \ **STYLING**: Henna Koskinen
MODEL: Emilia and Jonathan \ **YEAR**: 2009-2010
DESCRIPTION: All symbols, ufos, all the things we want to and should believe, or not.

TITLE: Rose Collection, Love Bag   **DESIGN**: Hoiming Fung & Baldwin Pui   **PHOTO**: Jacky Chee   **YEAR**: 2008
DESCRIPTION: This collection is an expression of romantic moments by highlight with a blooming rose. Holding a handbag will
feel like holding a rose(s). Love and Happiness are the elements we want to spread.

FASHION: Cooperative Designs \ **GRAPHIC**: Cooperative Designs \ **PHOTO**: Amy Gwatkin
STYLING: Elizabeth Cardwell \ **MODEL**: Siobhan Brewster \ **YEAR**: 2009
DESCRIPTION: Outsize Butterfly Jumpsuit and Butterfly Hoodie. The collection was based on peruvian imagery mixed with horror films faust and suspiria. Quirky patterns such as "dancing grannies" and outsized butterflies were combined with menacing witch knits. The collection was a combination of outsize fine knits with extra chunky handknits.

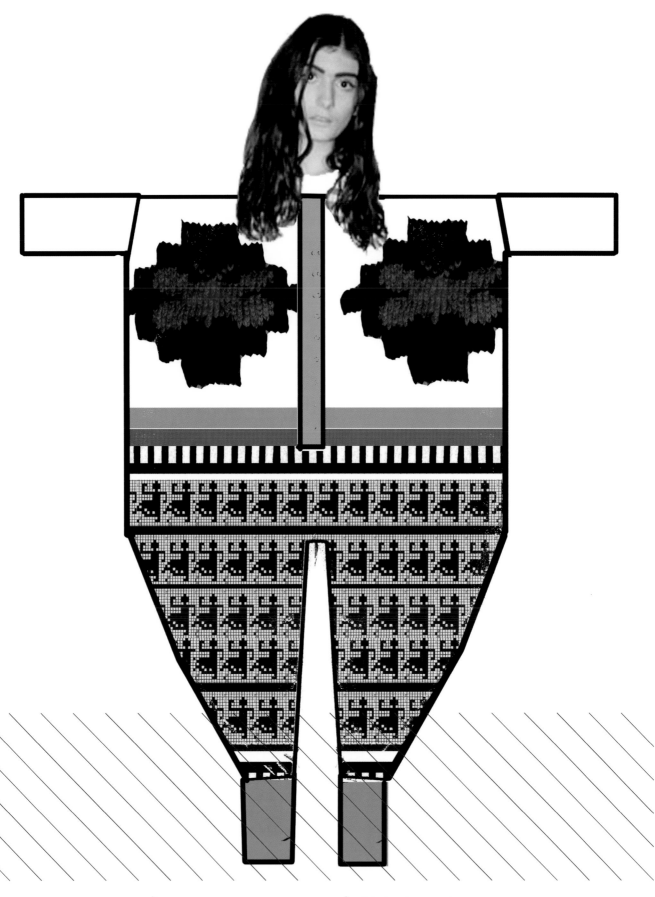

FASHION: Cooperative Designs \ **GRAPHIC**: Cooperative Designs \ **PHOTO**: Amy Gwatkin
STYLING: Elizabeth Cardwell \ **MODEL**: Siobhan Brewster \ **YEAR**: 2009
DESCRIPTION: Llama Hoodie with Dancing Grannies print.

TITLE: I Want to Believe \ **ART DIRECTION**: Daniel Palillo \ **FASHION**: Daniel Palillo
GRAPHIC: Laura Laine, Daniel Palillo \ **PHOTO**: Paavo Lehtonen \ **STYLING**: Henna Koskinen
MODEL: Emilia and Jonathan \ **YEAR**: 2009-2010
DESCRIPTION: All symbols, ufos, all the things we want to and should believe, or not.

TITLE: Branch necklace of the collection 'Season's Greetings'   **Design**: Martine Viergever \ **PHOTO**: Thomas Voorn
STYLING: Thomas Voorn   **MODEL**: Katinka, Matthijs   **YEAR**: 2008
DESCRIPTION: Branch necklace consists of real branches roughly tied to each other with silver string.

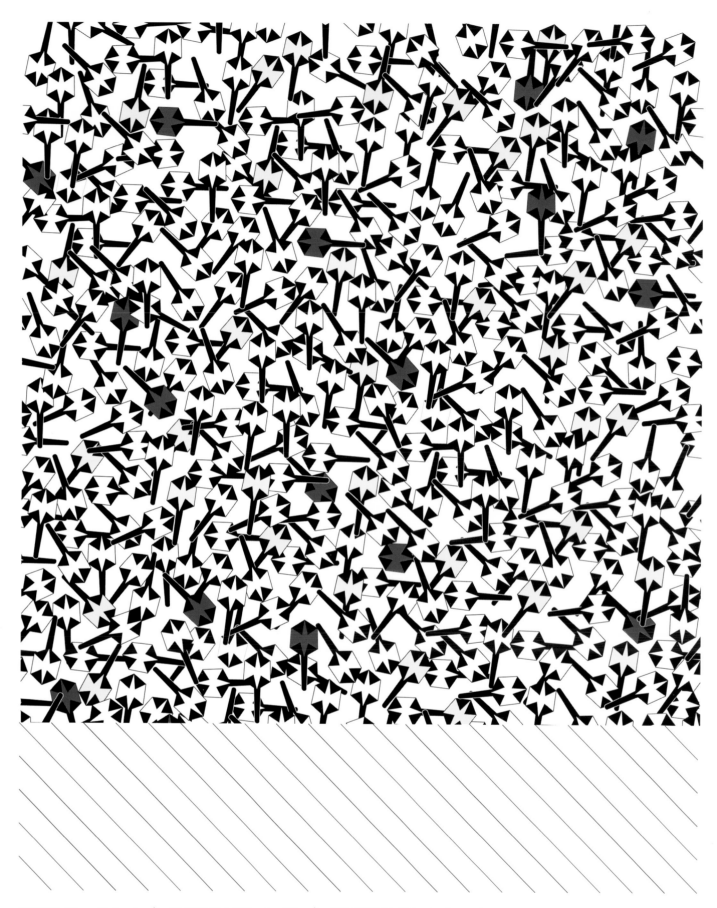

TITLE: Virus Collection \ **FASHION**: Kling by Kling \ **GRAPHIC**: Kling by Kling \ **PHOTO**: Studio SEEK
STYLING: Studio seek, Kling by Kling \ **HAIR**: Kling by Kling \ **MAKE-UP**: Kling by Kling
MODEL: Alexandra Blom \ **YEAR**: 2007

TITLE: Mod. Whatever by Polipo + 5PREVIEW \ **GRAPHIC**: Polipo + 5PREVIEW \ **PHOTO**: Giorgia Placidi
STYLING: Emeli Martensson \ **MODEL**: Emeli \ **YEAR**: 2009
DESCRIPTION: Collaboration between 5preview and the bicycle messenger bag brand POLIPO, high quality handmade bags.

TITLE: I Want to Believe \ **ART DIRECTION**: Daniel Palillo \ **FASHION**: Daniel Palillo
GRAPHIC: Laura Laine, Daniel Palillo \ **PHOTO**: Paavo Lehtonen \ **STYLING**: Henna Koskinen
MODEL: Emilia and Jonathan \ **YEAR**: 2009-2010
DESCRIPTION: All symbols, ufos, all the things we want to and should believe, or not.

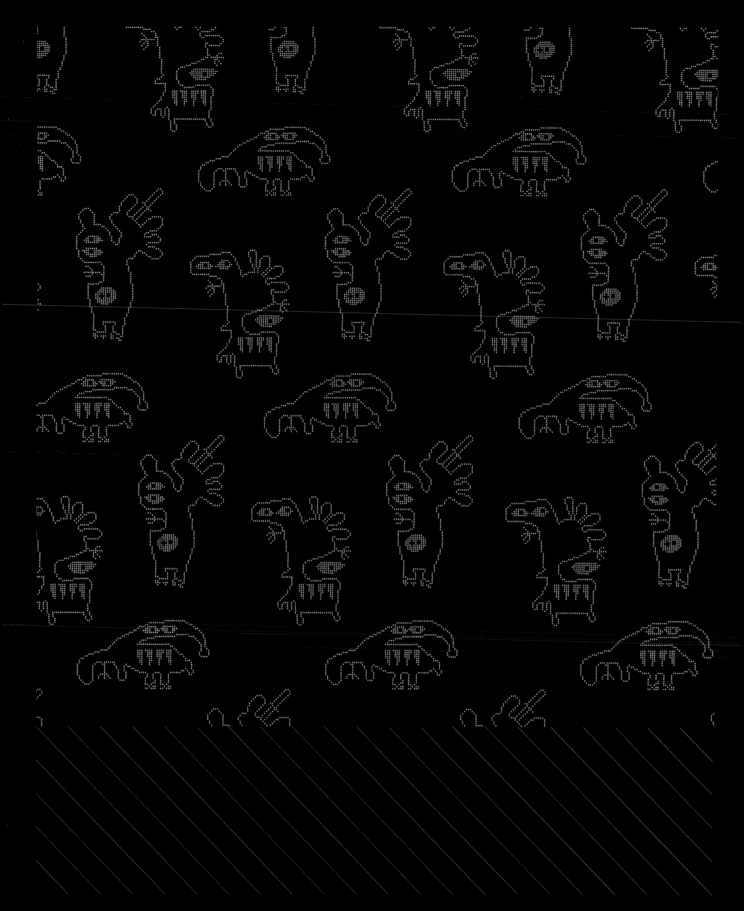

TITLE: Bestiario Collection   **FASHION**: potipoti   **GRAPHIC**: Nando Cornejo & Silvia Salvador   **PHOTO**: Hanayo
STYLING: Nando Cornejo & Silvia Salvador   **MODEL**: Jacky   **YEAR**: 2007
DESCRIPTION: Scary monsters uhhhhh!

TITLE: Cold outside & warm inside, Twiggy, Helicopter of the collection 'Season's Greetings'   **DESIGN**: Martine Viergever
PHOTO: Thomas Voorn   **STYLING**: Thomas Voorn   **MODEL**: Laurens & Katinka   **YEAR**: 2008

FASHION: Sandor Lakatos   PHOTO: Tamas Dobos   YEAR: 2008

FASHION: Sandor Lakatos   **PHOTO**: Tamas Dobos   **STYLING**: Kata Florian & Judy Judas   **HAIR**: Robert Radinkovics
MAKE-UP: Csilla Kiss   **MODEL**: Sandor Lakatos   **YEAR**: 2008

TITLE: KLING CLOWN \ **FASHION**: Kling by Kling \ **GRAPHIC**: Kling by Kling \ **YEAR**: 2009
DESCRIPTION: KLING by KLING brings KLING CLOWN to town! Come and experience a moment inside the mind of the Kling Circus. Stories to be told, expressions to be exposed, times to share behind the curtains.

INTERVIEW

Cooperative Designs \ UK

Annalisa Dunn and Dorothee Hagemann met on the MA Fashion course at Central St Martins in London 2007, whilst both specializing in knitwear. Upon graduation they founded knitwear label Cooperative Designs. Cooperative Designs create modern innovative knitwear, subverting traditional techniques, silhouettes and forms.

The designers also consult for other labels. They have just completed their second season consulting for Hussein Chalayan, helping to create a sophisticated experimental knitwear range, and have been supported by the British Fashion Council with New Generation sponsorship and have held catwalk presentations during London Fashion Week for two seasons.

F \ Annalisa and Dorothee are the designers of Cooperative Designs. What made you start working together?
C \ We met whilst we were both studying at Central St Martins on the MA. We both wanted to have our own businesses, and we got on well so we decided to give it a go. It has been great to have a business and design partner, we can support each other and we think it gives the collections a broader feel; there is twice as much thought, concept and work put into each piece!

F \ How do you cooperate with each other?
C \ We have been working together for two years now, so it has become quite a smooth process. We both tend to work separately, then we come together and discuss ideas and edit etc. So far we have always been on the same track. We also work with other designers on the collections, bringing in new elements. We have worked with jewellery designers, printers, prop designers, bag designers and embroiderers.
We also consult for other labels, most recently Hussein Chalayan for A/W 09/10.

F \ Strong graphics are showing on your fashion. Did you have a graphic design background before becoming a professional fashion designer?
C \ No, we have both always worked within fashion. Our graphics are influenced by Bauhaus and constructivism: merging photography, graphic design and painting.

F \ How do you define your style? Who is your target audience?
C \ Our style is handcrafts mixed with graphic pattern and a strong concept, to create a modern and fun aesthetic. Our target audience is fashion lovers who love craft, pattern and knit, but don't take themselves too seriously.

F \ You just made your London Fashion Week debut. What did you see and how did you feel?
C \ We met so many buyers and press, who were really supportive and excited by what we are doing. It is so encouraging to get that kind of support. We have also been supported by the British Fashion Council. They have helped us to take our collections to Paris Fashion Week and have introduced us to so many great people.

F \ You have done very nice pieces of women's knitwear so far. Will we see men's wear from Cooperative Designs in the future?
C \ We would love to! We did some menswear for British label SOAR, which was a great experience. Our graphics would translate well to menswear, so it is definitely something for the future.

Sandor Lakatos \ Hungary

Sandor Lakatos, born in 1981, is a Hungary bespoke tailor and menswear designer. Growing up in the environment of family owned fashion business and being greatly influenced by the excellent technicians, the designer made it clear early that fashion was his passion and would be his profession in his entire life. Starting in the year 1996, Sandor Lakatos has improved his techniques and perfected his knowledge. That creating new cut which is never seen before is his motivation and sometimes causes him a few sleepless nights.

F \ What type of designer are you?
S \ I'm menswear designer.

F \ How did your family business influence you in your career?
S \ It was no question, when I was child, I knew what I would be, because I felt me home in our family factory.

F \ You made yourself a T-shirt when you were only six. What was that t-shirt like?
S \ It was hand made, white and tight.

F \ You have been making and designing men's wear. Have you ever designed clothing for women?
S \ Of course I make sometimes, but not for sale.

F \ What are you doing in your sleepless nights?
S \ My ideas coming and coming and I have to write them down in my book.

F \ Do you have stockist anywhere in the world?
S \ I have my own studio and a boutique in Budapest.

hoiming \ Hong Kong, China

hoiming always explore new possibilities to carry things; thus, creating bags with reasons and surprises. While designing bags, it always challenges the notion of the usage, and how it relates to the body of the user. Its spirit is to explore and to inspire, and its works recapture the essence of elegance, in its own mischievous way. Hoiming Fung and Baldwin Pui are co-founders of "hoiming". Hoiming aspires to the hand-stitched leatherwork, which, to her means perfection and haute couture. Baldwin has worked in Hong Kong and Preen in London, and his works have a direct thematic inspiration that comes from daily life, which mirrors culture and society.

F \ Hoiming and Baldwin are co-founders of the brand Hoiming. How did you start working together?
H/B \ We have "worked" together since we were studying in college. We would assist and discuss to each other on projects even we were in different discipline.

F \ With a background of graphic design, Hoiming co-operates with you in making accessories for fashion showpieces. Baldwin, how do you think of Hoiming's design and what do you like her the most as your partner?
B \ I always believe in her senses and concepts. Her great ability on graphic together with her fine craftsmanship which easily help to present my ideas into 2D or 3D forms, and can always give me surprises.

F \ Baldwin's works have a direct thematic inspiration coming from daily life, and mirroring culture and society. Hoiming, how have you been influenced by your partner Baldwin?
H \ I believe we have always shared same attitudes on exploring styles, themes and ideas. We are not influencing each other on aesthetic area, but in fact that we are building it up together. The way that Baldwin has influenced me a lot would be his optimistic character, while I'm quite cautious. We can balance each other by having extreme working patterns.

F \ What was the inspiration behind Heavy Bag?
H/B \ This bag is made for a fashion show of Baldwin in April 2006. He liked to present the idea of "funny horror" movie so that I came up an idea to make a chain-ball bag as accessory. The "58kg" means special to me because I have been told by doctor that it should be my "standard average weight" according to my height...and it is how I feel about the recommendation.

F \ Your recent collection Pinocchio shows a chain of rose design, elegant and adorable. How did you start designing the collection?
H/B \ It started from a little puppet. One day we found a vintage little Pinocchio in the market. It reminded me that I couldn't remember any details of the film from the old time, although we can still easily tell the story to the children. Then we watched back the film from 1940, and decided to share that wonderful meaning behind to all others who have also forgotten long time ago like us. We also inspired from the lyrics of the very touching song "When you wish upon a star" from Pinocchio.

F \ You attended the Paris Fashion Week in March and must have had a great time. Can you share the experience?
H/B \ It was our 2nd time attended the Paris Fashion Week. It's a great platform to present our designs to the world within a short period of time. It also provides chance to meet with other designers from different countries. It's better to know the world by being there!

Daniel Palillo \ Finland

Daniel Palillo is a Helsinki based designer. His clothes doesn't rely on any ideology, but a result of spontaneous action and open mind. Signature for the collection is a tragicomic, a sense of dark humor and oversized shapes. The collection is both for men and women. For now his clothes are available worldwide in selected shops.

F \ You began studying fine arts when you were at the University of Arts and Design Helsinki, but changed to fashion design. What made you change?
D \ I felt that I needed to do clothes.

F \ You collection line is something between Gothic, hip hop and heavy metal. What is Daniel like in person?
D \ Daniel is a big mess, too many things going on all the time. So, may be that is something similar to my clothes.

F \ Who do you design for? Have you ever had any unexpected admirers?
D \ I design only for myself. Yeah I have a weird grandma who likes it.

F \ We have seen that your collection has some scary print on it, which just perfectly match your clothing concept. How do you work with your graphic designer?
D \ It depends a lot on who is the person I am working with.

F \ Your oversized baggy line has been very salable. What you think is the magic to make it work?
D \ I have no idea.

F \ What has been the best for you so far?
D \ Being able to do things that make me happy.

potipoti \ Germany

potipoti is a collaboration between two designers, Silvia Salvador and Nando Cornejo. Operating from Berlin (Germany) and Spain, potipoti creates fashion, graphic design, visual arts and product design.

The story of this duo begins in Salamanca, a university town in Northern Spain where both were graduating in Fine Arts. The studio-label potipoti was founded in 2005. Their distinctive aesthetic for graphics is reflected in their fashion designs.

The label manufactures its fashion products in small and reliable textile companies from Castilla y Leon (Spain) and Portugal, and they can be found in selected stores around the world.

F \ You have attended the March Paris Fashion Week and must have had a great time. What did you see and how did you feel?
P \ We presented our latest AW09 collection at Rendez Vous Paris. The feedback has been very good and Paris is always a fantastic place to spend a few days, even if you have a lot of work.

F \ Silvia and Nando both graduated in Fine Arts. After working in Madrid for a period of time, you both moved to Berlin in 2001. What was the motivation for the move?
P \ We´ve been living in Berlin since 2001. At the time, we only planned a summer holiday in Berlin, but stayed until today! We knew the city a little bit, because Silvia studied at Weissensee Art School for a year, in 1999. At that time, Berlin was not as hot as it is now, and we constantly had to convince our friends to visit us here. Berlin has been our home for the past eight years. We love the creative scene, and the energy that breathes in the streets.

F \ You did not choose to be artists but designers. What do you enjoy the most being designers while you might have never had that feelings being artists?
P \ We both studied Fine Art and come from a Graphic Design and illustration background. Our fashion is always strongly connected with Graphic Design. We love experimenting, and always have a lot of fun! We are self-taught fashion designers who have fun with the motto ´Do it yourself! With each collection we learn something new. We also tend to have a bit of distance from the fashion world, which helps to make our collection fresh every season.

F \ The application of your graphic design on fashion products is simple and changeable. Where do you usually get the inspiration?
P \ Contemporary and popular art in all its facets, folklore, street art, graffiti and music. We draw inspiration in small details, walking down the streets exploring, or being inspired by people with a knack for fashion. We also get a lot of inspiration through traveling, the further away, the better! This summer we wanted to go to a Pacific Island called Potipot. Our summer collection is inspired by this island.

F \ How does Potipoti keep fresh in such a fierce competitive environment?
P \ Being ourselves. We don't like to follow trends; we find more and more amusing to do what we feel like doing every time and being consistent with our own work without fear to experiment. We hope it will be more fun than it is now. We miss a certain sense of humor in fashion. We like to think that there aren't prejudices when it comes to clothing and people will dress with more personality.

Index

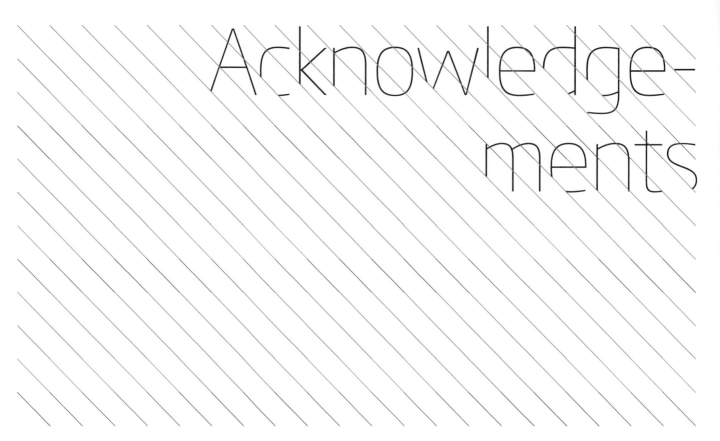

Acknowledgements

Thank you so much to all the designers who contributed to this book and their time for interview. Many thanks to all the creatives, photographers, illustrators, stylists and models who provided fantastic imagery and an opportunity to witness their creativity. Special thanks to Hanna Werning, Emeli Martensson, Paola Ivana Suhonen, and Karolina Kling for their writing of the four seasons. A massive credit to Zhao Yu and Angel for brilliant art direction. Thanks are also to many others whose names do not appear on the credits but made specific input and support for the project from beginning to end.